I FELT LIKE
I WAS FROM
ANOTHER PLANET

WRITING FROM PERSONAL EXPERIENCE

Norine Dresser

Addison-Wesley Publishing Company
Menlo Park, California • Reading, Massachusetts • New York
Don Mills, Ontario • Wokingham, England • Amsterdam • Bonn
Paris • Milan • Madrid • Sydney • Singapore • Tokyo • Seoul
Taipei • Mexico City • San Juan

Dedication

For my darling and delightful grandchildren—
Leila,
Zachary,
Avidan,
Isa.

May you and all children find joy
in discovering what is hidden inside of yourselves
through the magic of writing.

This book is published by Innovative Learning, an imprint of Addison-Wesley's Alternative Publishing Group.

Senior Editor:	Lois Fowkes
Design Manager:	Jeff Kelly
Production Manager:	Janet Yearian
Production Coordinator:	Claire Flaherty
Cover and text design:	DagenBela Graphics
Cover illustration:	Rick Garcia

Copyright © 1994 by Addison-Wesley Publishing Company, Inc. Printed in the United States of America.
ISBN 0-201-86058-9

5 6 7 8 9 10-ML-03 02 01 00

TABLE OF CONTENTS

PREFACE

"Describe a time when cultural differences caused a problem for you in this country."

In October 1989 I assigned this topic to three composition classes for non-English speakers at California State University, Los Angeles. At times humorous and always moving, the stories crystallized painful, embarrassing, life-turning moments; as soon as I read them I recognized the value of having students write about entering the new, often baffling culture of the United States. Writing gave students an opportunity to examine their pasts and, through the process of composing, gain perspective and distance between themselves and their learning experiences, however painful. Distancing is necessary for anyone trying to overcome traumatic experiences. Perhaps these tales could help others find freedom through writing from personal experience.

I also recognized that the stories are filled with significant social data. Their gripping disclosures could be of interest to those who might be unaware of the struggles that newcomers have. Furthermore, they mark a meaningful moment in U.S. immigration history: the prelude to a new multicultural society. No longer Euro-centered, these newcomers bring fresh influences and cultural riches from all over Asia and Central America. As time passes, memories become clouded, and events are forgotten. My compulsion to collect these still-vivid tales, now numbering in the hundreds, was the genesis for this book.

I Felt Like I Was from Another Planet contains fifteen tales relevant to students in grades four through eight. The stories were written by students struggling to master English—so different from their own native languages of Vietnamese, Chinese, Cambodian, Spanish, and Japanese—and I have made minimal changes; I have attempted to preserve the authenticity of the students' voices while providing solid writing models for other learners.

Many people have encouraged me with this work, and I would like to acknowledge them. First, I thank my colleagues at California State University, Los Angeles, who not only patiently listened to my ideas but participated by assigning the topic to their students: Lise Buranen, Virginia Crane, Chloe Diepenbrock, Marilyn Elkins, Jayasri Hart, William Hart, Nancy Hutcheon, Buddy Roberts, Arpi Sarafian, Sharon Smartt.

In addition, I am indebted to my consultants—those who answered questions about customs and beliefs or who supplied feedback from their professional points of view: Cameron Golestaneh, Dr. Teri Keeler, Emma Louie, Bunny Rabiroff, Maryam Rostani, Amy Sharafi, Leila Sharafi, Dr. Frances Cattermole-Tally and the UCLA Archive of American Popular Beliefs and Superstitions, Betty Woolf, Fay Zachary, Fahim Zand.

Then there are the dear friends who have held my hand through all my projects: Janice Garey, Kay Enell, Morris Polan, Jan Steward. I am beholden to you all and especially to Montserrat Fontes, who graciously gave so much time for valuable input and a close reading of the manuscript.

Next, there is the homefront support. I appreciate my brother Mickey Shapiro's enthusiasm for my ideas. I am grateful to my children, Mark Dresser, Andrea Berk, and Amy Dresser, and my mom, Bea Shapiro, who understood when I didn't have time to talk to them or when I talked too much about this project. Most of all, I praise my husband, Harold, who not only blessed my endeavors but was the unfortunate recipient of behind-the-scenes grumbling and the real me.

Of course, *I Felt Like I Was from Another Planet* would never have become a reality without Lois Fowkes, Senior Editor at Addison-Wesley's Alternative Publishing Group. She shared my fascination with the stories and recognized their value for students growing up in a multicultural society. Lois carefully and sensitively guided me through the publishing process, and it has been a nurturing experience.

Finally, I would like to thank all the students who have entrusted their experiences to me and most particularly the student writers of the wonderful stories in this book.

ANGELICA ARELLANO

YENTAM CHAU-TRAN

KIU P. CHU

ALMA ELIZABETH AYON MARTINEZ

PATRICIA ELIAS

LORENA E. GUZMAN

COLLEEN VAN HY

RAYMOND KWONG

NHI HONG LY

YEN LY

NAOMI NISHI

CHENG SOK PHE

MARIA RAMIREZ

DENISE THAI

TAI TRINH

I FELT LIKE I WAS FROM ANOTHER PLANET:
Writing from Personal Experience

PURPOSE

The first goal of *I Felt Like I Was from Another Planet* is to develop the authentic writing voice of students in grades four through eight. *I Felt Like I Was from Another Planet* guides students to draw from their pasts (no matter how limited) to express their feelings and experiences. This helps them build confidence in their writing skills, a necessary tool for success in school and in society. The second goal is to heighten students' sensitivity to living in a multicultural world.

The fifteen story models present information, issues, and emotions students can relate to. Students respond to the human dilemmas and conflicts caused by cultural differences. They are asked to identify with the story characters, to describe and empathize with characters' feelings, and to project themselves into the situation by filling in words or drawings inside open heads called Headlines/Open Minds. Through a series of questions they actually become part of the story. They are asked what characters might be thinking or feeling. Sometimes they are asked to predict what will happen to the characters in the future. Other times they are asked how the characters and their actions make them feel or how they might have responded in a similar situation. By answering these questions, students gain insights into themselves and into the behavior of others, an important process for any writer.

Through follow-up questions, discussion, and uncomplicated exercises, students create their own related stories. They translate their personal experiences into written words, communicate their stories through art by means of drawings or cutouts from magazines, or transform their stories into dramatic presentations. In addition, they evaluate each other's work, then revise and edit their own writing. Finally, they are given an opportunity to preserve and circulate their work by publishing it, instilling a sense of pride in their accomplishment of writing about the value of their own experiences.

The story models were written by college students at California State University, Los Angeles. However, the time frame for the incidents goes back as far as the fourth grade, indicating the power of the events that have remained so colorfully intact in their memories. Although most stories were written by students from Asian and Latino backgrounds, the backgrounds should not be the primary focus. Instead, the universality of the issues should be addressed, so that students can see that experiences and emotions are similar, even though background, customs, diet, appearance, and language are not.

Emphasizing similarities will help set up a commonality among students in a multicultural classroom. Even in homogeneous classrooms, *I Felt Like I Was from Another Planet* can heighten student consciousness about ethnic diversity by exposing students to the issues of a multicultural society.

To heighten appreciation for cultural differences, each unit has sections called Cultural Background and Cultural Relativity Questions that deal with culturally specific data. Students look within themselves to discover how they contain culturally relevant material. Through classroom exchange of information, they will deepen their appreciation for their own ethnic and family heritage and recognize parallels between their own customs and those of their classmates.

HOW TO USE THIS BOOK

Many suggestions for how to use this book are provided. What follows are merely recommendations, and you are invited to be as creative as possible in adapting them to your specific needs. Ideally, each writing project should be carried out over a period of 5–7 days to give students a chance to absorb and reflect on ideas presented in the unit, critically assessing whether their own experiences are the same or different. Extending the length of time from the beginning of the unit until the writing of the last draft will increase the significance of the final writing product.

PRE-WRITING

1. Start with the Warm-up Questions to encourage a variety of responses and focus attention on the subject matter so that students can perhaps anticipate the issues about to be explored.

2. Before you begin The Story, inform students that the stories are true experiences written by other student writers. Depending on students' reading abilities, you may choose to read the story aloud while they listen and follow along on the handout, have students read the story themselves, or have students read with a partner.

Have students underline phrases or words they find important, memorable, or confusing, or give students some self-sticking tags and have them write down and attach their thoughts, questions, feelings, and contradictions as they move through the reading. This stimulates a dialogue with the characters and a commentary on the events.

Clarify any misunderstandings. A New Vocabulary list precedes each story, anticipating any potentially unfamiliar words.

The stories need not be presented in sequence. Any of them may be used when appropriate to curriculum or when related social issues arise. However, it should be noted that the stories at the end of the book deal with issues that may be more sophisticated and challenging, such as male and female roles and prejudice. Subject Matter and Issues lists precede each story to help you find units suitable to your needs.

3. Immediately following the reading, have students respond to the content by writing inside the open heads of the Headlines/Open Minds handout. Tell them to imagine what the characters in the story felt and thought. Limit the time to five to ten minutes to stimulate spontaneity and encourage gut reactions. Then ask students to share some of their responses, or put students into small groups to exchange responses with one another before opening up the discussion. Ask students what they might have done in a similar situation.

It is exciting when students begin making connections between the story characters and themselves. By requesting that students project their own feelings onto the characters, the open heads offer a nonthreatening way to face fears, to express ideas, to experiment with trying on the feelings of others. Students less adept with words may first want to draw pictures that they can explain later. Asking students to explain why they wrote or drew what they did offers them an opportunity to examine and express their own motivations.

4. Opinions and Ideas should be expressed orally to demonstrate that people interpret situations differently and that questions do not necessarily have definitive answers. To express creativity, students are also asked to hypothesize about alternative outcomes. With this section you might want to divide the class into five groups and assign each group just one question to discuss among themselves before opening up a full classroom discussion.

Note: Steps 5–8 are recommended to get maximum use of this book. However, if there are time restraints, you can eliminate either one or both of the Follow-up Activities as well as the sections on Cultural Background and Cultural Relativity Questions, moving directly to the Discovery Draft Phase Two.

5. Two Follow-up Activities are offered to reinforce the message within the story as well as to build other classroom skills in language arts. For example, retelling the story in their own words allows students to change from first to third person when writing the narrative. Other kinds of individual and small-group activities include role playing, creating comic strips and ads, analyzing television programs and fairy tales, and conducting surveys and interviews. Activities used in one unit can often be interchanged with other units and can be adapted for class use or outside credit. The techniques can also be used as variations for writing original stories.

6. The Cultural Background section provides further examples of the subject matter and practical information that may be used to expand students' knowledge about other people's customs. Share with your students whatever you feel is appropriate. In general, the information gives cultural background that may explain why characters in the stories ran into trouble or how their native traditions caused conflicts in this society. Although the story models were written by students from Asia and Latin America, discussion can be expanded to include customs from all over the world.

7. Cultural Relativity Questions stimulate class discussion and demonstrate cultural variation. Here the objective is to have students explore their own backgrounds to give parallel information to be shared with their classmates. Pick and choose questions you feel are appropriate or most relevant to your classroom situation. Students can answer these

questions on their own or in small groups, or they can interview each other. If they are unsure of the answers, they can interview their parents and return to the classroom with the information.

8. Pursuing extra credit oral or written reports on the topics listed in the Learning More section helps students build skills in English, social studies, and library research. A bibliography is included in each unit to direct you to resources beyond standard reference materials.

DISCOVERY DRAFT
Phase One—Oral Storytelling

Several topic alternatives for you to choose from are given in each unit. However, it is preferable that students be given no more than two choices, and often it is better to have them all writing on the same topic. Go over the topics carefully and make sure students understand what is being asked.

Divide your class into groups of four to five. Have each group discuss among themselves which of their own experiences might make a good story. Next let them tell these stories to each other. It will be rare for every student within a group to think of something this fast, but usually there will be at least one person in each group who will think of a possibility, and that is good enough to serve as a model for the group.

Have each group share their stories with the entire class to help those who still might not have any ideas generate something on their own. Explain how these oral versions will bear great resemblance to the written form. Reassure them that since they already know how to tell stories orally, writing them will be a familiar process; there is always at least one character that something happens to, and there is a beginning, a middle, and an end. Discovering that they are already experienced in communicating their experiences orally from a first-person point of view will give students confidence to write from a first-person point of view.

Phase Two—Written Storytelling

Sometimes it is useful to have a one-day break between the oral telling of the stories and the actual writing, particularly if students haven't decided what to write about. The break gives them a chance to think about the topic. If students seem unsure of themselves, encourage them to talk to family members about their story ideas.

Since this is a discovery draft, it is best not to give too many instructions or restrictions. Let students first get their ideas down on paper; save the refinements, sharpening of focus, and embellishments for the revision processes. Time restrictions and your students' skills will determine the required length of writing time or number of paragraphs or pages.

There is a Telling Your Own Story Variation for each unit. Sometimes these suggestions are interchangeable between units. The age and skill level of your class will determine their use.

Assessment and Revision Processes

Three different forms of assessment are described. You may use any or all three forms, or you may add another stage. Rewriting should follow each assessment session.

It is useful to ask students to keep all drafts of their work and to number and date them. This will make their progress apparent, and they will see that writing is an ongoing process.

STUDENT REVISING

After students have finished their Discovery Drafts, you may give them a copy of the Writer's Checklist on page xxi, or you may choose one or more of the following directions to guide students in improving and expanding their own work.

1. Identify a clear beginning, middle, and end of the story.

2. Add dialogue to the story.

3. Write your story from another character's point of view.

4. Reinforce a particular mood, emotion, or feeling.

5. Establish the characters and setting. Use lively adjectives and adverbs.

6. Clearly identify cause and effect.

7. Clearly identify the problem.

8. Make your sentences different lengths.

9. Add sensory details.

Point out that sensory details refer to sight, sound, smell, taste, and touch. Explain that the simplest way to add sight details is to include the names of colors—that when a writer uses the word *red*, readers see red in their minds.

Sometimes it helps to put an example on the board. Write, "She bought a car." Then add "... red car." Add "... a red car with black leather seats and a black leather top." Finally, add that the car was customized with a "white thunderbolt design on the doors." Stress that with each added detail, readers' minds receive a more accurate and lively picture. Tell students that other sight words can relate to brightness or darkness, shape or size. Ask them to give you some examples of these kinds of details.

For sound details, show students how they can use words that imitate sounds (*pop* or *bang*) or words that imply sounds (*crash* or *smash*). The other senses may be more difficult, but *rough* or *smooth* denote texture, and other good examples of touch are *soft, wet, dry, damp, hot,* and *cold*. For smell and taste, give students examples of the power of mentioning the fragrance of certain flowers (roses, gardenias, carnations) or trees (pine, lemon, eucalyptus) or the smell and taste of an ocean breeze; suggest brainstorming flavors, such as salty, sweet, bitter, sour, minty, smoky.

You will only need to give an in-depth discussion of sensory details once in a semester. The Writer's Checklist will reinforce students' awareness of this requirement for good writing.

PEER EVALUATION

Peer evaluation can be an effective way for students to provide positive feedback to each other. It also allows them to see both strong and weak models of their classmates' writing. In this manner, they learn to apply the positive aspects to their own writing and eliminate or correct problems similar to those in the weaker papers.

You may elect to use peer evaluation with each writing unit, or you may use it only occasionally. Three variations are given below.

Method One

Have two or three students trade papers and answer the following questions on a separate piece of paper.

1. What did you like about the story?

2. Can you circle the beginning, middle, and end?

3. Which is your favorite part?

4. What would you change in the beginning? middle? end?

5. How could the story be improved?

Method Two

Divide the class into groups of four for a read-around. Have students block out their names and write the last four digits of their phone number on the top page of their own papers for identification. Then collect the papers from each group and pass them to the next group to read. After each person in one group reads a complete set of papers (or looks at a group of drawings) let the group choose their favorite, write down its identification number, and give three reasons why they liked it.

When each group is finished, have them pass the batch of papers to the next group and repeat the procedure; ideally, each group reads all groups' papers except their own. If time is limited, have students read at least two groups of papers.

Afterward, ask each group to give you the identification numbers of their favorite papers and put them on the board. Talk about the reasons why the papers were selected. Emphasize that students should remember the strengths of these papers when they revise and edit their own.

Method Three

Have each student read her or his paper to a partner and see whether the criteria on the Writer's Checklist have been met.

TEACHER ASSESSMENT

When you go over the papers and write comments, focus on the content rather than on the writing mechanics. It is more useful to ask questions in the margins (Why were you so frightened? Can you describe how the house looked?) than to correct errors. In this way students are more positively guided into revising their work.

If you are able to confer individually, you may want to have students read aloud from their own work, which often enables them to hear their own mistakes or omissions. In addition, it is valuable to focus on only one writing issue, such as sequence or character description, with each conference.

Special Note: If you confer with Asian students, it is best to avoid yes/no questions. Their tradition often dictates that they express an understanding of what the teacher means even when they do not. If they were to indicate nonunderstanding it would cast aspersions on your teaching ability, and they will not want to offend you. Therefore, instead of asking, "Do you understand?" (which students are culturally obligated to answer yes), ask them to tell you or show you what they don't understand.

FINAL DRAFT

Depending on time restrictions, students can write final drafts in class and in the process ask for assistance from you or from their classmates, or they may finish the writing at home. Make sure that students title their work.

PUBLISHING

As students become more proficient they may develop their writing to the point that they want stories typed and illustrated. The class stories can be bound so that students will have a memory of their own and each other's experiences. This will be an accomplishment for students and, in turn, their stories can become models for subsequent classes. Have students keep their original copy for their notebooks and ask for a duplicate for the classroom book. Leave the final page empty for students to autograph and dedicate messages to each other. If you elect to publish your students' writing, I would appreciate receiving a copy of their stories.

TEACHING TIPS

Many of the comments listed after particular units may be used with other units. Suggestions help you direct attention to the significance of the stories and underlying issues. While your impulse may be to bring closure to each unit, it is equally important to emphasize that these issues are timeless dilemmas for all human beings. The problems may never be completely or satisfactorily resolved. Issues that occur in almost every story are:

▲ The problems of being an outsider and the emotional pain that this causes

▲ The fear of outsiders and their unfamiliar ways

▲ The rewards of learning about other people's traditions

Specific issues and the units in which they occur are listed below.

ACCEPTING SOMEONE WHO IS DIFFERENT FROM YOURSELF
Holidays (Unit 1); Food Taboos (Unit 2); Prejudice (Unit 15)

BEING CAUGHT BETWEEN PARENTS' OLD WORLD CUSTOMS AND AMERICAN CUSTOMS AND VALUES
Physical Contact (Unit 7); Females and Males (Unit 14)

BEING EMBARRASSED BY PARENTS
Audience Response (Unit 10)

BEING KIND TO A STRANGER
The Hidden Meaning of Colors (Unit 4); Prejudice (Unit 15)

CULTURAL ADAPTATIONS THROUGH IMITATION AND TRIAL AND ERROR
Holidays (Unit 1); Clothing Customs (Unit 3); Table Manners (Unit 5); New Year's and Luck (Unit 6); The Influence of Heredity (Unit 9); Audience Response (Unit 10); Teachers and Students (Unit 12); Family Life (Unit 13)

CULTURAL RELATIVITY—NOT BEING JUDGMENTAL ABOUT OTHER PEOPLE'S WAYS
Food Taboos (Unit 2); The Hidden Meaning of Colors (Unit 4);
Table Manners (Unit 5); New Year's and Luck (Unit 6); Rites of Passage (Unit 8)

EMOTIONAL PAIN IN BECOMING ACCULTURATED
Holidays (Unit 1); Clothing Customs (Unit 3); The Hidden Meaning of Colors (Unit 4); Physical Contact (Unit 7); Audience Response (Unit 10); Games (Unit 11); Teachers and Students (Unit 12)

GOING AGAINST PARENTS' RULES
Physical Contact (Unit 7); Females and Males (Unit 14)

HARDSHIPS OF IMMIGRATION
Holidays (Unit 1); Clothing Customs (Unit 3)

INFLUENCE OF CULTURAL RULES AND CUSTOMS THAT HAVE BEEN INFORMALLY AND UNCONSCIOUSLY LEARNED AND ACCEPTED, YET RARELY QUESTIONED
Food Taboos (Unit 2); Table Manners (Unit 5); New Year's and Luck (Unit 6); The Influence of Heredity (Unit 9); Family Life (Unit 13)

REASONS FOR IMMIGRATION
Holidays (Unit 1); Clothing Customs (Unit 3)

REWARDS IN LEARNING ABOUT OTHER PEOPLE'S TRADITIONS
The Hidden Meaning of Colors (Unit 4); New Year's and Luck (Unit 6).

STANDING UP FOR SOMEONE ELSE
Holidays (Unit 1); Prejudice (Unit 15)

STANDING UP FOR YOURSELF
Holidays (Unit 1)

STEREOTYPES
Females and Males (Unit 14); Prejudice (Unit 15)

UNDERSTANDING PARENTS' DIFFICULTIES AS IMMIGRANTS
Audience Response (Unit 10); Females and Males (Unit 14)

WHAT IS ACCEPTABLE AND APPROVED IN ONE CULTURE CAN BE OFFENSIVE OR UNACCEPTABLE ELSEWHERE
Food Taboos (Unit 2); Clothing Customs (Unit 3); Table Manners (Unit 5); Physical Contact (Unit 7); Rites of Passage (Unit 8); The Influence of Heredity (Unit 9); Audience Response (Unit 10); Teachers and Students (Unit 12); Family Life (Unit 13); Females and Males (Unit 14)

XENOPHOBIA
Holidays (Unit 1); Prejudice (Unit 15)

SOURCES

A list of sources appears at the end of each unit. Some of them provide information for the Cultural Background section and can be used for Learning More research. Others contain ideas for Follow-up Activities. A large portion of the data comes from my own unpublished research.

HANDOUTS FROM BLACKLINE MASTERS

The following sections are printed on separate pages so that they may be duplicated for student use:

▲ Stories

▲ Headlines/Open Minds

▲ Writer's Checklist

The Writer's Checklist reinforces the basic requirements of a story and pinpoints details that should be included to help students become more proficient writers.

WRITER'S CHECKLIST

Does your story include characters?

    Who are they?

    How old are they?

    How do they look?

    How do they act?

    Why do they act that way?

    What do they feel? Why?

Does your story have a setting?

    Where does it take place?

    What does that place look like?

    When does the story take place?

Does your story include action?

    What is the conflict?

    How does it come about?

    How is it resolved?

    How are the characters affected?

Which sensory details have you included?

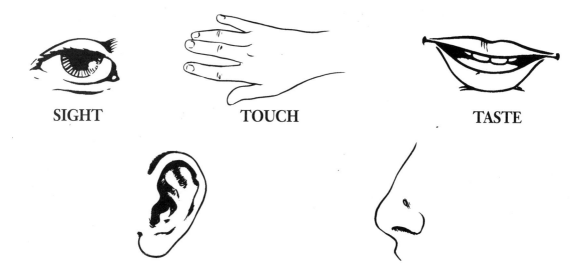

SIGHT   TOUCH   TASTE

SOUND   SMELL

UNIT ONE

HOLIDAYS

NEW VOCABULARY
Communists
violate

SUBJECT MATTER
Holidays
St. Patrick's Day

ISSUES
▲ Accepting someone who is different from yourself
▲ Cultural adaptations through imitation and trial and error
▲ Emotional pain in becoming acculturated
▲ Hardships of immigration
▲ Reasons for immigration
▲ Standing up for someone else
▲ Standing up for yourself
▲ Xenophobia

WARM-UP QUESTIONS
▲ Have you ever been in a classroom where other students were mean or unfriendly to a new student?
▲ How do you celebrate St. Patrick's Day?

My name is Helen. I was born in Cambodia and was raised in a family that was able to provide me food, education, and happiness. However, due to the Communists and starvation, I lost my parents, sister, and brother. I lost the most important persons in my life, especially my mom and dad. Tell me, what is the use of living in a country like this? Why did my beautiful motherland turn out to be like this? I had to escape my country, but it wasn't easy at all. It caused pain, starvation, thirst, fear, and danger.

I still remember how joyful it was to experience the happiest moment of my life when I arrived in the United States. That was the time I got to smell fresh air, drink clean water, have enough food to feed my stomach, and of course live in a peaceful world and be able to stay away from bullets flying across my head almost every day. It was good to feel that I was safe.

The most exciting day was my first day of school in the U.S. because in Cambodia I was too young to attend school. Every day I would count off the days left before school started. March 17 was my first day of school, and it was also Saint Patrick's Day. Saint Patrick's Day is an Irish holiday when in my new American city everybody is supposed to wear green because green means a good luck color. If you don't wear it, it means that you violate the rules, so therefore people will pinch you. Well, poor me. I didn't know anything about wearing green.

I was so enthusiastic to meet my teacher and to find out what school was like. Unfortunately, school turned out to

I Felt Like I Was from Another Planet

be the opposite of what I was expecting. When I first entered my classroom, the teacher introduced me to the class. She told them my name was Helen, but I was ignored due to the fact that I didn't speak English and the way I was dressed. I was wearing a blue skirt and a white blouse which my sister made by hand. That was the way students dressed in my country. I guess that the American students thought that I was wearing some kind of uniform.

The teacher guided me to my new seat, and as soon as I took my seat everyone looked at me and I felt like I was from another planet. As the teacher walked away from me, my classmates started to pinch me. At first it started off with one person, then two, three, four and everybody else started running from their desks and pinched me. I was so scared, and didn't know what was going on. I knew that I was a big girl and shouldn't be crying in class. I tried to control my temper and at the same time I tried to stop myself from crying. I lost my patience because it was so painful and both of my arms had bruises all over. That's when I decided to pinch them back. Then the teacher screamed so loudly at the class to be quiet and leave me alone. It was so quiet that the whole classroom could hear me sobbing and the teacher's footsteps walking toward me. She pinned a green leaf on my blouse and guided me to the rest room. It was so embarrassing that from then on I always kept my distance from everyone. It wasn't until the fifth and sixth grades that I began to make some new friends.

Now I am in college, but I still remember my first day of school and Saint Patrick's Day. Sometimes when I think about it I begin to laugh, even though it was the most embarrassing day of my life.

HEADLINES/OPEN MINDS

Write your answers inside the heads of the characters. You can use words, phrases, or pictures.

1. How do you think Helen felt going to her first day of school? List some of her feelings.

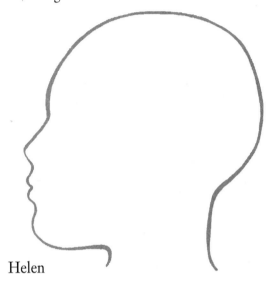

Helen

2. What do you imagine Helen was thinking when her classmates began pinching her? List at least three thoughts.

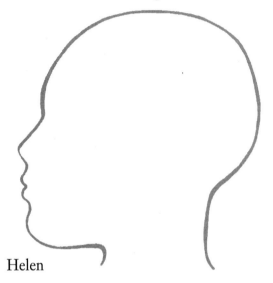

Helen

3. What were some of your feelings when Helen's classmates began pinching her?

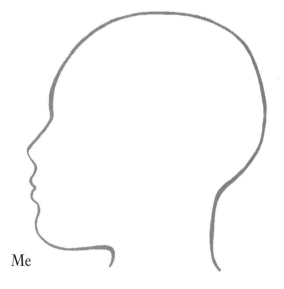

Me

4. What were some of your thoughts when Helen began pinching the other students?

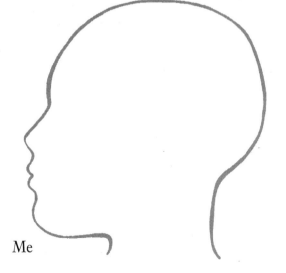

Me

OPINIONS AND IDEAS

1. If pinching is a St. Patrick's Day tradition at this school, were the classmates right or wrong for pinching Helen? Explain your answer.

2. Did the teacher handle the situation well? Explain your answer.

3. After this incident why do you think it took a year before Helen was able to make new friends?

4. Have you ever been mean or unfriendly to a new student? Explain your answer.

5. How did you feel the first time you didn't have on something green for St. Patrick's Day? What happened to you?

FOLLOW-UP ACTIVITIES

1. Make a comic strip. Show Helen's unhappy St. Patrick's Day. Make a different box for each of the following scenes. Add balloon dialogue for each speaker.

[box 1] The teacher introducing Helen

[box 2] The children pinching Helen

[box 3] Helen pinching back

[box 4] The teacher pinning the green leaf on Helen's blouse

[box 5] Your own ending to the story

2. Write a letter to someone who is planning to visit the United States. Tell about one American holiday custom that might surprise that person. (Suggestions: April Fool's Day, Halloween, St. Valentine's Day, Thanksgiving.)

CULTURAL BACKGROUND

The American celebration of St. Patrick's Day reflects the influence of the large number of Irish immigrants arriving here in 1845–1849, escaping from the potato famine in Ireland. They brought with them their belief in their patron saint, St. Patrick, who among other deeds and miracles is thought to have rid Ireland of all its snakes.

Irish immigrants, like the Cambodian immigrant in this story, were discriminated against when they first arrived. Eventually they became part of mainstream America, and St. Patrick's Day is now celebrated by Irish and non-Irish Americans. The U.S. celebration has become more elaborate and commercial than St. Patrick's Day in Ireland.

In Ireland, St. Patrick's Day is both a national and religious holiday, a quiet family day. Most people attend church and outside you can buy something green to pin on clothes, such as shamrocks, badges, or ribbons. Ordinarily the Irish do not wear green clothing on this day. Unlike in the U.S., if someone forgets or chooses not to wear any green, nothing happens.

The Irish celebration contrasts sharply with the celebration in the U.S., particularly in American cities such as New York, Boston, Chicago, and San Francisco, where they have large parades. Parties are held throughout the U.S., and people serve a traditional Irish meal of corned beef, cabbage, and potatoes. At homes and in restaurants people serve green beer, green gelatin, green mashed potatoes, green milk, green doughnuts, and cake with green icing. Most important, people wear something green—usually clothing—though green make-up, lipstick, and even hair may also be seen. Those who don't wear green, even if they're not Irish, may be scolded or pinched.

In general, holidays or calendar customs fall into categories—to celebrate heroes (Martin Luther King, Benito Juarez, George Washington, St. Patrick); to commemorate historical events (end of a war, signing of the Declaration of Independence); to show appreciation for a family member (Mother's Day, Father's Day, Boy's Day in Japan); to celebrate a religious event (Las Posadas, Easter, Passover).

CULTURAL RELATIVITY QUESTIONS

1. How do you celebrate St. Patrick's Day?

2. What holidays does your family celebrate?

3. Which is your favorite family holiday?

4. What do you do on this holiday?

5. Has a friend ever introduced you to a new kind of holiday? Which one was it?

6. Is there any holiday that you are curious about and would like to find out more about? Which one? Why?

7. If you celebrate April Fool's Day, what kinds of pranks do you play? What pranks have been played on you?

8. If you celebrate Christmas, when do you open your gifts?

9. If you celebrate Fourth of July, what kinds of activities do you participate in?

10. If you dress up for Halloween, what has been your favorite costume?

LEARNING MORE

The following related topics may be explored: St. Patrick; the Potato Famine; Irish immigration to America; Irish customs and symbols (leprechauns, shilelaghs, shamrocks, Irish harp, kissing the Blarney stone). Other ethnic-associated holidays: Hanukkah; Kwanzaa; Chinese New Year; Obon Festival; Día de los Muertos; Juneteenth.

TELLING YOUR STORY

Choose one.

▲ Tell about a favorite holiday that you and your family celebrate.

▲ If you could create a holiday to honor a person who has never been honored before, who would you choose and why?

TELLING YOUR STORY VARIATION

Choose one.

▲ Alone or with a partner, create a new holiday. Make a poster announcing the name of this holiday, when it will be celebrated, where it will be celebrated, and the special events that will take place.

▲ Choose to honor either your mother or father and make a coupon book of gifts that you can give that won't cost money. Make at least six coupons and decorate each one. For example, make a coupon for Take Out the Trash; Wash the Dog; Pull Weeds from the Yard; Fold the Laundry; Cook One Meal; Wash the Car.

TEACHING TIPS

For the Warm-Up questions, encourage students to talk about any first day of school, even their most recent one.

Tie in the idea of the starving Irish with the starving Cambodian girl.

Discuss the following questions:

▲ What are some of the conditions that cause people to leave their native homes? (religious or political persecution; war; lack of economic opportunities; forced immigration, such as slavery)

▲ How difficult is it to leave friends, family members, and possessions and move to a place where everything is different, unknown, unfriendly? A good follow-up question might be to ask students what one possession they would take with them if they were suddenly forced to leave their current homes for another location far away. This provides an opportunity to talk about objects with symbolic meaning, those objects that represent family and home and security.

Ask students if they know why their parents, grandparents, great-grandparents, or great-great-grandparents came to this country. If they don't know, have them interview some family members to find out.

Address this issue: Why is it that when a stranger enters a room, the first response of others often is to treat that stranger with either suspicion, fear, or hostility? Introduce the concept of xenophobia, fear of strangers. Explain that xenophobia is universal, and can lead to acts of violence, even war. However it is possible for individuals to learn to overcome xenophobia by focusing on similarities among human beings rather than differences— especially physical differences.

Ask if Helen's classmates pinched her because she was also a newcomer. Did Helen's newness give them extra pleasure in the pinching? Is there any way that Helen's first day of school might have been made less traumatic?

Raise the following questions: Suppose an alien from outer space were to walk into this room. What would you do? How would you feel? How would you respond? How many would actually be friendly to the alien?

Depending on the grade level, you might want to conduct an experiment by arranging for a stranger to sit in on your class while you proceed with your normal routine. Afterward ask students how they felt when the stranger entered or how they felt with the stranger sitting among them. Were their feelings and thoughts mostly curious, friendly, worried, or hostile? Explain that all these feelings are normal, but also indicate that there are risks in reacting in a negative way. For example, they might miss an opportunity to meet someone interesting or make a new friend. They might hurt that stranger's feelings and later on, they might discover that that stranger was in a position to hurt them.

Another issue you might want to raise is what it feels like to be alone and attacked. When does one stand up for oneself and fight back? When does one become a good Samaritan? What are the risks of doing this? Why are people often reluctant to step in and help?

In discussing holidays, students will find that even if they celebrate the same one, family traditions and ethnic variations exist. The Cultural Relativity Questions are designed to reveal these similarities and differences. Pay tribute to the differences. Assure students that there is no right or wrong way to celebrate. In addition, unusual ethnic or regional holiday customs can be explored: Day of the Dead, Leif Ericson Day, Laguna Indian San José Day, Cheyenne Frontier Days.

SOURCES

Cohen, Hennig, and Tristram Potter Coffin. *America Celebrates! A Patchwork of Weird and Wonderful Holiday Lore.* Detroit: Visible Ink, 1991.

Martinez, Jimmie, and Arlene Watters, eds. *US: A Cultural Mosaic: A Multicultural Program for Primary Grades.* 823 United Nations Plaza, New York, NY 10017: ADL of B'nai B'rith, n.d.

FOOD TABOOS

NEW VOCABULARY

Benares	reincarnation
Hindu	sacred
Indian	taboo
processions	

SUBJECT MATTER

Food taboos among different cultures
Ganesh
Indian customs
Symbolic role of food

ISSUES

▲ Accepting someone who is different from yourself
▲ Cultural relativity—not being judgmental about other people's ways
▲ Influence of cultural rules and customs that have been informally and unconsciously learned and accepted, yet rarely questioned
▲ What is acceptable and approved in one culture can be offensive or unacceptable elsewhere

WARM-UP QUESTIONS

▲ Are there certain foods that you are not allowed to eat because of your culture or religion?
▲ Have you ever offered some food to a friend and he or she was not allowed to eat it?

The Birthday Party

I am Gloria, and although I was not born in Mexico, my parents were, and they taught me Mexican culture and customs. During my senior year in high school I met a new friend whose name was Viji. We got to be pretty close, and she was very nice and caring. She was from India, and she was the only close friend I ever had from that country.

Viji's birthday fell on a Sunday in July and we agreed to celebrate it together on Saturday. I planned everything. We would go to my house and eat dinner with my family and a couple of other close friends. After dinner we would go dancing for a while and just have a great time.

All that Saturday morning my mother and I spent the day cooking and cleaning the house. My mother prepared this terrific barbecued roast. She made Mexican rice and corn. She also made a salad and fresh biscuits and a pomegranate punch. I made this wonderful tasting strawberry cake. It was just divine, of course, because I made it.

My friends arrived at 4:30 P.M. and we sat down to eat dinner at 5:00 P.M. The table looked great and so did everyone there. Then everything started to go wrong. As we were all sitting down ready to eat, my father asked us all to hold hands to say our blessings. Viji looked around and leaned over to ask me what we were doing. I responded by telling her we were giving thanks to God for our food. She said that she didn't do that at her house and asked if it was OK if she didn't give her blessing, so I said, "Sure." However, I noticed my father looking at my friend, and he seemed a little uncomfortable. Finally, my mother uncovered the food and started to serve. I noticed Viji staring at the food. She asked me what everything was and how it was prepared. She then leaned over again and

I Felt Like I Was from Another Planet

told me that in her house they didn't eat beef and that she didn't either. It was against her religion. In India the cattle were considered to be sacred. All of a sudden I felt this cold sensation running through my body. I didn't know what to do. I excused myself from the table and called my mother into the kitchen and explained the whole situation.

I noticed Viji feeling uncomfortable but at the same time she was trying to be nice and not spoil the dinner. Well, my mother came up with an idea. At the dinner table she tasted the roast, then claimed that it was too salty, took it to the kitchen and ordered some take-out fried chicken.

At this point I noticed that my father was having second thoughts about eating dinner at all. Well, we ate dinner anyway and it turned out OK. My mother then cleared the table and brought out the delicious cake I had made, and we sang "Happy Birthday" to Viji.

As we were eating the cake Viji explained to everybody about her cultural background and the reasons why she and her family didn't eat beef. She told us she was from the city of Benares and that she and her family are Hindus. Viji explained that she did not eat beef because cows are considered sacred and Indians try to protect their milk supply.

Viji also believed in reincarnation. She told us that she didn't believe in the God we prayed to, but she believed in one of their gods who had the head of an elephant. In India they had parades or grand processions to celebrate this god and real elephants would be covered with fine costly robes and jeweled harnesses. She said that some were painted in bright colors.

This was perhaps one of the weirdest experiences I've ever had. I felt very awkward not having known this important information about my friend before. However, I did learn that the next time I invite someone over for dinner at my house I should first find out everything about their culture and tell them about mine, as well. Fortunately, the night ended up great. We all went dancing and just had a blast!

HEADLINES/OPEN MINDS

Write your answers inside the heads of the characters. You can use words, phrases, or pictures.

1. How do you imagine Viji felt while watching Gloria's family say their blessing and eat the meat? List two or more feelings.

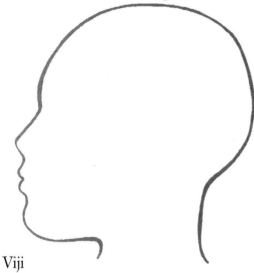

Viji

2. What do you imagine Gloria's father was thinking when he saw Viji refuse to say the blessing?

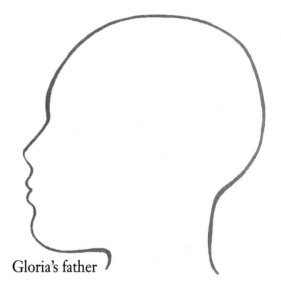

Gloria's father

3. How do you imagine Gloria's father felt when his wife took away the meat and ordered the chicken?

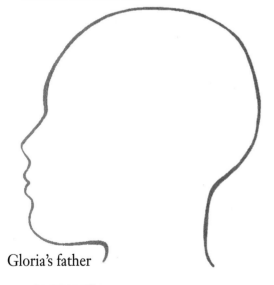

Gloria's father

4. How do you imagine Gloria felt when her mother said the roast was too salty?

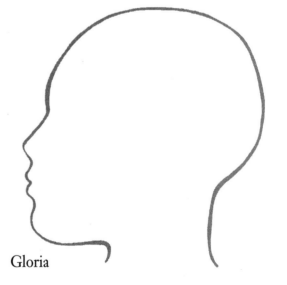

Gloria

OPINIONS AND IDEAS

1. What kind of a person is Gloria? Why do you think this?

2. What kind of a person is Gloria's father? Why do you think this?

3. What kind of a person is Gloria's mother? Why do you think this?

4. Do you think Gloria's mother handled the situation well by removing the beef and ordering the chicken? Why or why not?

5. Is there some other way that she might have solved the problem? Describe it.

FOLLOW-UP ACTIVITIES

1. Watch television on Saturday morning or after school and carefully observe three to five TV food commercials. Answer these questions.

▲ What kinds of foods are being promoted?

▲ Is the food really good for you?

▲ Is this food the same kind that your mother would buy for you even if you didn't ask her to? Explain your answer.

▲ What kind of person is telling you about the food? (Another child? An entertainment figure? A cartoon character? A sports star?)

▲ What do these food advertisements tell you? What are the messages? Do you believe them? Should you believe them? Why or why not?

▲ What kind of food habits are being promoted? Do they promote good health habits or bad health habits?

2. In words and pictures, create an advertisement for one of your favorite foods. Draw or cut and paste pictures from magazines. Through your advertisement tell why this food is so appealing—its taste and nutritional value.

CULTURAL BACKGROUND

Taboos

One man's meat is another man's poison. This proverb sums up the phenomenon of food preferences and abhorrences. Food taboos have always served as markers separating different groups of people. Focusing on a food that is foreign to us is nothing more than a subtle way of delineating "them" from "us" and therefore is a convenient way to maintain barriers between humans. This is the result of learned food habits that occur early in life involving ideas about what is good, what is bad, what is clean, and what is unclean. These ingrained attitudes are very difficult to change. Contrary to folk belief, taboos are created less for hygienic and health purposes and more for cultural, economic, and ecologic reasons. The power of the taboo is so great that if a person unknowingly eats a taboo food and later discovers it, or is forced to eat a taboo food, the revulsion that follows is so powerful that it can cause illness (hives, diarrhea, dermatitis) and even death.

For Hindus, there is no greater sacrilege than killing a cow because the cow is thought to be the mother of life. In India love of cows affects life in many ways. Cows are regarded as members of the family and are adorned with garlands. People pray for them when they get sick and call in neighbors and a priest to celebrate the birth of a new calf; government agencies maintain old age homes for them. Thus, to eat this venerated animal would be an abomination. Mohandas Gandhi wrote a constitutional law preventing this occurrence.

In the United States the most common food taboo is against eating dogs, which elsewhere are savored; for example, among the Aztecs of ancient Mexico, in the Caribbean countries of the past, in 19th century Paris, where recipes for dogs have been discovered, and in Asia today.

As a result of Americans' horror of eating dogs, during the 1988 Olympic Games in Seoul, Korean restaurants were advised to remove dog entrees from their menus in order to avoid offending American tourists. However, Americans' taboo against eating dog is not necessarily based on religious sanctions. It has more to do with the role of dogs in our society as "man's best friend," a family member who often shares the master's food and bed. American dogs are frequently treated to the best medical care and even costly burial ceremonies.

In this country and across the globe both Moslems and Jews have taboos against eating pork and shellfish. Melanesians will not eat stingray or bush pig; members of the Wind Clan of the Omaha Indian tribe are forbidden to eat or even touch shellfish. Ethiopian Christians must not eat camel meat, and in Mongolia, ducks are forbidden.

Ganesh

The Hindu god with the elephant head that Viji refers to in the story is called Ganesh. Here, in brief, is his story. The Goddess Parvati wanted a child, and her consort, Lord Shiva (another god), didn't want one, so Parvati made Ganesh, a perfect baby boy, from her own skin.

One day when Shiva returned home from a long voyage he found this unknown child guarding his wife's chambers. Parvati had told Ganesh to let no one in, so when Shiva tried to enter, the child refused to admit him. In anger, Shiva took his sword and lopped off Ganesh's head.

When Parvati discovered what happened, she screamed at Shiva, "That's our child!" Panicked, Shiva raced into the jungle to find a head to replace the one he had cut off. The first creature he encountered was an elephant, so Shiva chopped off the elephant's head and placed it on the neck of his son. That is why the god Ganesh is always depicted with the head of an elephant.

Ganesh is the most worshiped god in India. Most often he is called the Lord of Obstacles because he brings success, wisdom, and wealth. Ganesh usually wears a snake around his neck or middle and a jeweled crown atop his head. He frequently has four arms and carries a broken tusk in one of his right hands and a bowl of sweets in one of his left hands. This elephant-headed god is usually in the company of a rat who sometimes carries him around.

Ganesh has also been called the Lord of Books because Hindus believe he helped to transcribe the *Mahabarata* (the great Hindu epic). Thus he can be depicted wearing glasses and reading. During August, Ganesh festivals are held all over India, where celebrants create huge papier mâché statues of him dancing, seated on a throne, or seated on his rat.

CULTURAL RELATIVITY QUESTIONS

1. Is there some food that you are not permitted to eat because of cultural or religious beliefs?

2. Do you know of someone who has a different food taboo than you do?

3. Would you ever consider eating the following foods?

snake	liver	fried pork intestines
alligator	octopus	chocolate-covered ants
raw fish	tripe	stuffed cow intestine
goat	sheep's eye	stuffed sheep stomach
brains	tongue	grubs
grasshoppers	bear paw	buffalo

4. What are some unusual foods, regional foods, homemade foods, or ethnic foods you enjoy?

5. Are there certain foods that you must eat only on specific occasions?

6. Are there certain foods you must not eat on certain days or dates?

7. What is the most recent new food you have learned to eat and enjoy?

8. How are your food favorites different from your family's?

9. Do you have a favorite comfort food (something you like to eat when you are upset, sad, or anxious)?

10. In your family what food is given when you are sick?

LEARNING MORE

The following related food topics may be explored: food taboos; Indian festivals; Indian mythology and gods; Indian geography or history.

TELLING YOUR STORY

Choose one.

▲ Tell about a time when you had to eat something brand new and you were reluctant to try it.

▲ Tell about a time someone served you a food that was against your eating rules.

▲ Tell about a time when you offered someone something to eat that they weren't allowed to eat.

▲ Tell about a time when you wanted to try a food seen in a television advertisement, but when you tried it, it was not like what you expected.

TELLING YOUR STORY VARIATION

Choose one.

▲ Draw a picture of your favorite meal. Label each food.

▲ Make a menu of your favorite foods. Describe each item and draw a picture right next to it showing how it looks.

▲ Pick a partner. Pretend one of you is a food server in a restaurant and the other is a customer. The food server has to talk the customer into ordering a new or unusual food. (The server might want to select from the list on page 18.) Think up some benefits or positive aspects of the food. The customer can try to resist or be convinced. Act out your drama for the rest of the class.

TEACHING TIPS

Emphasize that emotional reactions to untried foods are common. This is part of learned behavior. As children, we absorb food rules from our parents and rarely question them. An adult student once revealed that she never ate chicken because as a child when she was offered chicken, her mother always admonished, "It's not on your father's diet!" The child had accepted this prohibition and never had questioned it. When this woman grew up she asked her father why chicken was not on his, and now her diet. The father explained that as a youngster he lived near a chicken farm and was traumatized by the daily slaughtering of chickens. His refusal to eat chicken was accepted by his wife and passed down to their children.

Discuss temporary diet restrictions students may be familiar with, such as during Lent or Passover, or times when certain special foods are eaten, such as Italians eating seven fishes on Christmas Eve.

It will be helpful to discuss the stereotypes of Indian life that most non-Indians have—that cows seemingly have more value than humans, or that cows overrun the country. You might tell students that there are many benefits to the large cow population. In addition to providing milk, cows provide low-energy substitutes for tractors and excrete about 700 million tons of recoverable manure, which is used for fertilizer and as a good source of cooking fuel. Cow dung is also used as a household flooring material. After death, cow skin is the source for India's large leathercraft industry.

Another issue to highlight is the symbolic role of food. To share food with another person is an act of trust. Breaking bread together is a powerful act of communion. Therefore to refuse food offered by another is equivalent to saying you don't trust them. This, in part, may account for the hostile response of Gloria's father to the girl who didn't worship his God and wouldn't eat the meat.

Open up a discussion about the difference in the ways that Gloria's mother and father reacted to the situation. Exploration into this area, while touchy, can be fruitful. It is a way of showing students that mothers and fathers may respond to situations differently and may not agree on domestic issues. In some households mothers may be more conservative; other homes may be more like Gloria's. Talk about the extraordinary sensitivity of Gloria's mother and her creative solution to the problem of what to do with the barbequed beef. Her actions revealed not only her concern for her guest, but also for how her daughter would be affected if Viji's religious rules were violated.

The first Follow-Up Activity helps students critically view television advertising techniques. It is designed to heighten awareness of being manipulated in order to increase sales for products that might even be harmful to health. This also provides an opportunity to bring up issues and principles of nutrition.

The second Follow-Up Activity can be carried out as written, but it is also possible to have the students themselves experiment with advertising manipulation techniques in order to "sell" their food products. In creating their ads they might try untruths, exaggeration, and false testimony from high visibility spokespersons. For this variation, it might be better if students work in teams of two or three.

SOURCES

Brown, Robert, ed. *Ganesh: Studies of an Asian God*. New York: SUNY Press, 1991.

Camp, Charles. *American Foodways: What, When, Why and How We Eat in America*. Little Rock, Ark.: August House, 1989.

Farb, Peter and George Armelagos. *Consuming Passions: The Anthropology of Eating*. Boston: Houghton Mifflin, 1980.

Sengupta, Uday Shankar, illus. *Color Me Ganesha*. San Francisco: Asian Art Museum of San Francisco, 1986.

UNIT THREE

CLOTHING CUSTOMS

NEW VOCABULARY

Communist

sponsoring

SUBJECT MATTER

Appropriate and inappropriate clothing customs
in the U.S.

Cross-cultural clothing customs

Hair fashions

Relationship of clothing and hair fashions to
societal issues

ISSUES

▲ Cultural adaptations through imitation and
trial and error

▲ Emotional pain in becoming acculturated

▲ Hardships of immigration

▲ Reasons for immigration

▲ What is acceptable and approved in one culture can
be offensive or unacceptable elsewhere

WARM-UP QUESTIONS

▲ Have you ever felt self-conscious because of the
clothes you were wearing?

▲ What do you know about the clothing customs of
other countries?

I could hardly hear my little tummy crying of hunger. It was cold and we were in a small boat that was crowded with 100 men, women, and children. For four days, our boat seemed to be nowhere. All four of us, my three brothers and I, were squeezed next to our mother. We had shortage of food and water but none of us could eat or drink because whatever we took in, we threw up.

Children were crying and men were screaming, "Throw them off and feed them to the sharks!" It was a nightmare. We were escaping Communist Vietnam in hope of finding a safe place to live peacefully. We were lucky that we got to stay in the camps in Hong Kong for a year, and six months in the Philippine Islands. Finally, there was hope. The news came that our aunt was sponsoring us to come to America, the land of the free, the richest nation in the world.

The plane landed. My aunt and her husband drove two cars to pick up the nine of us and take us to their home. That is when I decided to call myself the American name Tiffany. The very next day my aunt took us shopping at K-mart for new clothes. My mom picked out what I thought to be the most beautiful outfit that I ever saw. The price was $9.99. The outfit was white, covered with pretty red, yellow, and pink flowers. The shirt had two front pockets where I could put my hands for warmth. I couldn't have been happier, and I was all smiles all through the day.

One month later, my aunt took my brothers and me to register for school. We were so excited that we all wore our new clothes because we had never attended school before. Although I was nine years old, I was placed in the first grade. I thought I was the best looking kid in school with two long

I Felt Like I Was from Another Planet

pigtails that hung all the way to my small waist. I had on black cloth shoes, the kind that you might find in Chinatown, and I wore them without socks.

I entered the class and all eyes were shooting at my direction. All of a sudden, I felt like an alien from another planet. Even the teacher was staring at me with a funny look. I don't remember her, but the color of her hair was totally different from mine. To me it was like the color of the sun. I was so much smaller and shorter than all the other kids, but I felt even smaller right then. I wondered what made them so much bigger and taller than me.

The silence was broken by the teacher when she greeted me and guided me to an empty desk next to a dark-skinned girl with curly hair. She was very pretty with big eyes and long lashes. She smiled but I was speechless.

Moments later I saw someone of my culture talking to the teacher. Then that person, a female, approached me and asked in Chinese, "Why are you wearing your pajamas to school?" I didn't say anything and didn't understand why I wasn't supposed to wear what I was wearing to school. To me, pajamas are torn with patches and made of bad materials that make it uneasy for you to sleep in, not something that is so soft and comfortable that was 100% cotton.

I don't remember what happened after that very embarrassing day, but I never wore those so-called pajamas to school again. When I think back right now, the incident seems very amusing. How was I to know that it was wrong to wear what I wore to school that day? I guess it would be the same for anybody else from a totally different background.

HEADLINES/OPEN MINDS

Write your answers inside the heads of the characters. You can use words, phrases, or pictures.

1. What do you imagine Tiffany's thoughts were as she went to her first day at school?

2. What do you imagine the teacher thought when she saw Tiffany in her pajamas?

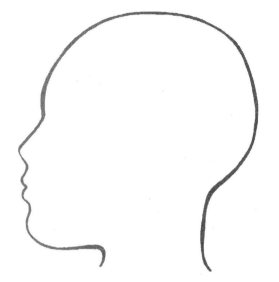

Tiffany

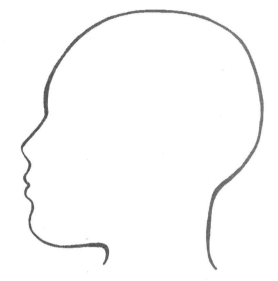

Teacher

3. What do you imagine the first graders thought when they saw Tiffany dressed that way? List at least four different thoughts.

4. How do you imagine the Chinese-speaking lady felt when she had to tell Tiffany that she shouldn't wear what she was wearing?

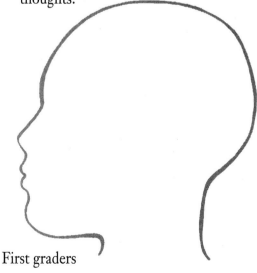

First graders

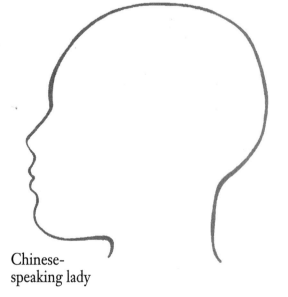

Chinese-speaking lady

OPINIONS AND IDEAS

1. How would you describe Tiffany's personality? Why do you think this?

2. How would you describe Tiffany's aunt? Why do you say this?

3. Would you ever be able to tell a classmate she or he was wearing the "wrong" kind of clothing? Why or why not?

4. How would you have reacted if you had been told you were wearing the "wrong" clothes to school?

5. Do you think it was easy or hard for Tiffany to get over this first day of school embarrassment? Why do you say this?

FOLLOW-UP ACTIVITIES

1. Look at a map and then draw a picture showing the route Tiffany's family took from Vietnam to Hong Kong to the Philippine Islands to the United States. Or make a map showing where your own family came from. Talk with your parents. Find out the route that family members took to reach America and to the city where you now live. Draw a map showing this.

2. Make a clothing catalog. Draw pictures or cut and paste clothing examples from newspapers or magazines. Tell what the item of clothing is, who wears it, and what occasions it is for—school, church, beach, a wedding, shoppping, a picnic, and so on.

CULTURAL BACKGROUND

Although many American private and parochial schools require that students wear uniforms, in public schools dress codes have become quite liberal. In the 1990s students can wear almost anything—girls can even wear shorts—but not pajamas. The issue is what is private and what is public clothing. Private clothing, such as underwear and sleepwear, is ordinarily not acceptable out-of-doors, especially at school. However, when pop star Madonna turned her underwear into outer wear on her 1990 "Blond Ambition" international concert tour, she started a fad that was eagerly seized and accepted as a new fashion statement. Tiffany was misled by the lovely soft cotton material of her outfit. As she explained, in Vietnam the best clothes are used for public wear and the poorer quality clothing is for inside the house. She is not the only one to be confused. Judy Chu, City Councilwoman for the city of Monterey Park, California, (a city with a large Chinese immigrant population) reports complaints from residents about older Chinese immigrant men wearing their pajamas out on the street. It is the soft fine quality of these garments that misleads the wearers into believing that the clothing is meant to be worn outside.

The word *pajama* comes from the Hindu *pyjamas*, meaning leg clothing. Pajamas were borrowed and adapted from India, but they did not become popular sleepwear in the U.S. until World War I. Up to that time most men wore nightshirts and women wore nightdresses. In the 1930s, specially designed pajamas were worn outdoors in fancy settings such as seaside resorts; they were made of elegant shantung or crépe de chíne. Unfortunately Tiffany and the elderly gentlemen of Monterey Park were 50 years too late in their fashion choice.

Marilyn Elkins surveys the world of ethnic literature and reveals the dilemmas that immigrants face when, like Tiffany, they are trying to enter mainstream culture and adapt to current fashion. She tells of the problems of a Native American woman who was sent to a white boarding school where all the girls had short hair. In the young woman's Native American culture, only mourners wore short hair (cowards wore shingled hair). Think of the conflict this caused for the woman. Her quandary is typical of the constant considerations that immigrants face when trying to fit into a new culture.

Fashion and clothing customs reflect societal issues. The 1960s were socially tumultuous times mirrored in experimentation with dress. Tied into the Civil Rights and "Black is Beautiful" movements, African Americans stopped straightening their hair and began wearing and valuing Afro hairdos for their natural beauty. African American men began wearing dashikis.

The popularity of the Beatles and their connection to Indian music and meditation inspired the Indian look in clothing—colorful flowing skirts, Indian bells and beads for women, Nehru jackets for men—and led to the acceptance of Indian textile designs of block printing and embroidery. In addition, there was the "granny" look with women in long dresses wearing wire-rimmed glasses. And during this time what hippie could be without his or her poncho, tie-dyed shirts, love beads, and patched bell-bottom jeans!

School dress codes also were in upheaval in the 1960s. Controversies swirled around the acceptable hair length for boys (authorities wanted it short) and the acceptable skirt length for girls (authorities wanted it long). Unfortunately, this was also the time of the miniskirt, causing constant confrontations between parents and children, and students and school administrators.

Another trend began. Women wanted to wear pants, but that brought resistance. This was not the first time that society had objected. In 1932 after the Paris Chief of Police spotted Marlene Dietrich wearing pants and a man's jacket while walking along the Seine, he ordered her to leave. In the 1960s, female employees wanted to wear pants suits to offices, and women teachers wanted to wear them in their classrooms. However, many bosses and principals refused permission. Further, certain restaurants would not seat women dressed in pants. A story spread about a fancy restaurant that refused service to a customer because she was wearing a pants suit. Unruffled, the patron went into the restroom, removed her pants and wore only her top which barely covered her underwear, yet she was now considered acceptably dressed and escorted to her table.

Blue jeans are perhaps the most representative piece of American clothing. They are the invention of Levi Strauss, a Bavarian-born Jew who emigrated to the U.S. in 1848. He became a peddler and en route to San Francisco from New York took bolts of canvas that he hoped to sell to the miners as tents. Alas, it was the wrong kind of canvas. However, Strauss discovered that the canvas was just the right kind of sturdy material for pants that could hold up under the harshness of mining life. The miners were desperate to have such a piece of work clothing, so they each paid six dollars in gold dust for tailoring one pair of stiff rugged pants. These became the very first Levis, which changed the world of fashion. At a later time Strauss switched from canvas to denim, dyed it indigo blue, and in 1870 he added the trademarked copper rivets. Since that time Levis have become a symbol of the American West and are worn the world over.

Although clothing customs are generally the same across the United States, variations exist, generally affected by religious rules. Among certain Orthodox Jewish sects, men wear black suits, beards, and side curls (*paises*). Their wives cover their hair with wigs, wear long sleeves, and usually have skirt lengths longer than what is in fashion.

Amish clothing is mostly homemade. The Amish use buttons on men's shirts, trousers, and underwear and on children's dresses, but hooks and eyes are required on men's coats and vests. Men's trousers are like sailor pants, called "barn door britches." Females of all ages wear a *kapp* (prayer veil), head coverings tied at the neck, with bonnets over them in winter and for full Sunday dress. Men of all ages cover their heads with straw hats in summer and black felt hats in winter. Adult males must wear the *mootsa* to church, a coat with split tail. They must have beards, but no moustaches.

While American blue jeans have affected clothing styles all over the world, the U.S. has absorbed clothing customs from other people as well. Moccasins were taken from Native American garb; non-African Americans wear cornrow hairdos; Americans wear Japanese *zoris*, Mandarin collars, Japanese *kimonos*, Mexican *rebozos*, Hawaiian *muu muus*, and Eskimo *mukluks*.

Although Western dress tends to dominate clothing customs in cities around the world (in rural areas traditional garb may predominate), there are still places where national costume prevails, especially in India. Here women prefer to wear the *sari*, six to nine yards of colorful cotton or silk, worn over a tight-fitting, half-sleeved or sleeveless bodice called a *choli*. Regional differences dictate the variation in the way the sari is draped. Many city men wear Western garb, but there are others who don *kurtas*, long loose-fitting shirts generally knee length that are worn over *pyjamas*. Costume variations occur in different regions.

National clothing is often still worn in many countries: Indonesian women prefer to wear the *sarong* (a wrap-around skirt of cotton batik) and *kabaya* (a jacket-like blouse). Men in the Bermuda Islands wear Bermuda shorts. Filipino men wear the *barong*, a loose, often pleated front white or cream-colored shirt worn outside the trousers. In tropical Latin American countries, men wear something similar called *guayabera*. Nigerian women wear wrap-around skirts of bright cotton batik prints, *iro*, and tops, *buba*; the men wear *daishikis* (shirts) with embroidery on the fronts and sleeves. They also wear three-piece outfits of solid or print cotton or linen, consisting of a top, *ajbada*, undershirt, *buba*, and straight-legged pants, *sokoto*.

In Middle Eastern countries women must be covered by the *chador* (a shapeless piece of clothing to completely cover the body from head to foot). This rule is common in places such as Yemen, Saudi Arabia, Iraq, Iran, and Jordan, where women must cover everything except their hands, feet, and face. In some places women also cover their faces with a very thin veil or wear a mask that reveals only the eyes. Indoors a woman may loosen her hair and be less completely covered, but only in the presence of a husband, brother, son, father, or other women.

After the overthrow of the Shah in 1979, the Ayatollah Khoumeini proclaimed that women in Iran had to return to wearing the black *chador*, and he outlawed the light-colored or print ones that were popular during the time of the Shah. The Ayatollah also ruled that men could no longer wear neckties, a symbol of the West, or short sleeves, T-shirts, and shorts in public. When men wore dress shirts, the top button had to be fastened so that no hair would show, the hair being a sign of sexiness.

Elsewhere, people may wear their national garb daily or only on festive and ceremonial occasions as they choose. In Scotland, clan gatherings require that members wear tartan kilts, woolen skirts for men in the plaid representing their clan membership. According to the rules for correct dress during the day, the tartan kilt is worn with a tweed jacket and vest. The kilt, which reaches the center of the knee cap, should be belted around the waist and is never worn with suspenders. A *sporran*, a large leather pouch, suspended from the waist and covered with fur and tassels, is worn in front of the kilt.

Cross-culturally it is easy to make mistakes about clothing, just as Tiffany did. At one time bright blue ceramic bead necklaces imported from the Middle East were a very popular form of costume jewelry in the United States. However, one day while I was wearing one of these necklaces, an Iranian student began laughing at me. At that very moment I discovered the reason those necklaces were called donkey beads. In Iran they were used to decorate the donkeys and no human would ever consider being similarly adorned.

Roger Axtell relates a similar incident in which a woman created an amusing (not for her) situation by incorrectly wearing ethnic jewelry. She had been in Togo and purchased beads that she thought were quite beautiful. To her dismay, she later learned that the beads she was wearing around her neck were to be worn at the waist to hold up a loin cloth.

CULTURAL RELATIVITY QUESTIONS

1. Do you or does anyone in your family have native clothing from another country? What kind? When do you wear it?

2. In your family, is there a special way women or men are supposed to wear their hair?

3. Does anyone in your family have a piece of ethnic jewelry or heirloom jewelry? Describe it.

4. In your family, at what age are girls allowed to wear makeup?

5. Does your family care if the older boys have moustaches or beards?

6. In your family, are boys allowed to have long hair?

7. In your family, what would happen if you dyed part of your hair green?

8. Does anyone in your family have a tattoo?

9. Does your family choose the clothing you wear?

10. Does your family have rules about skirt lengths, sleeve lengths, boys going without shirts, or the wearing of bathing suits?

LEARNING MORE

The following related topics may be explored: clothing customs in other countries; history of costume in the U.S.; national costumes; folk costumes; women's fashions; men's fashions; hairdo customs; body ornamentation: tattooing, face painting, scarification; textiles—what kinds of materials are used for clothing; history and geography of silk, wool, cotton, animal skins, synthetics.

TELLING YOUR STORY

Choose one.
> ▲ Tell about a time when you had to tell someone he or she was wearing something inappropriate.

▲ Tell about a time when you wished someone had told you what to wear for a special occasion (birthday party, Easter egg hunt, piñata party, scavenger hunt, amusement park, Halloween, dance).

▲ Tell about a time when someone criticized or made fun of clothing you were wearing or the way you wore your hair.

TELLING YOUR STORY VARIATIONS

Choose one.

▲ Show and Tell: Bring an item of ethnic or antique clothing, jewelry, or hair ornament belonging to a family member or friend. Tell your classmates where it comes from; on what occasions it is/was used; how old it is; how the owner obtained it, and as much about it as possible. Point out design features.

▲ Design a new item of clothing for boys or girls, women or men. It can be futuristic, practical, fantastic, or make a political statement. Give this piece of clothing a name, then name the design after yourself and affix your label.

TEACHING TIPS

This unit provides an opportunity to appreciate cultural differences as they affect the manufacture and use of objects. Through some of the activities it is possible to show how ordinary everyday items such as clothing and jewelry can provide lessons in history and culture.

One idea to convey is that clothing customs are not fixed and rigid; they are constantly changing. Thus, it might be possible that in the future pajamas will be acceptable school wear. For example, who would ever have predicted that sweatsuits and athletic shoes, formerly worn only in gymnasiums and out on the field, would become fashionable wear in classrooms, restaurants, movies, or at the shopping mall?

Discuss how fashion can be examined in the context of societal issues, but that those who accept the new fashions get caught up in controversy. For example, hair is frequently a subject of contention for both men and for women. The controversy can be over hair length, hair style, hair color, facial hair, or body hair.

I have been to two different funerals of elderly women whose eulogies referred to their courage by being the first ones in their families to bob their hair during the 1920s. To have cut one's hair at that time was a mark of an independent woman rebelling against restrictive rules for females. This brought familial and social censure at the time, but admiration 70 years later.

Have students interview members of an older generation to ask them about conflicts they had with their parents about wearing new hairstyles. Who won? How were family relationships affected? What did the argument signify to them or to their parents? This could turn into a lively classroom discussion encompassing history, social change, and going against parents' and society's rules.

You might also want to consider peer pressure influencing clothing choices. Ask students if their friends have ever talked them into buying or wearing something that they weren't sure about or something their parents didn't approve of.

The first Follow-up Activity is a good exercise in geography as well as family history. It offers an opportunity to talk about the reasons why families migrate and helps develop empathy for other immigrants, showing how human needs for freedom and economic survival are universal.

Bring in the opposite concept. African American immigrants came here as slaves. How would that affect them? What happens if a person is brought against his or her will to labor in undesirable working conditions? What happens when family members are deliberately separated?

Reinforce the idea of how difficult it is for immigrants when they first arrive, and point out that without language skills they are unable to even ask questions, the answers to which might spare them embarrassment as revealed in the story.

If students do the first Telling Your Story Variation, regardless of how well or how poorly the clothing fits, you may want to have them wear their items as if they were in a fashion show.

SOURCES

Axtell, Roger E. *Gestures! Do's and Taboos Around the World.* New York: John Wiley and Sons, 1990.

Chu, Judy, City Councilmember, Monterey Park, California. "Challenges for Chinese Americans." An unpublished plenary speech given at the Conference on Chinese

Americans (28 August 1992), California State University, Los Angeles.

Elkins, Marilyn. *Fashion. The Oxford Companion to Women's Writing in the United States.* New York: Oxford University Press, 1993.

Gehman, Richard, and William Albert Allard. "Amish Folk." *National Geographic.* 128:2 (August 1965): 227–253.

Harrold, Robert. *Folk Costumes of the World.* Pool, Dorset, England: Blandford Press, Ltd., 1984.

Hostetler, John A. *The Amish.* Scottdale, Penn.: Herald Press, 1982.

——————. "The Amish in American Culture." *Historic Pennsylvania Leaflet No. 12.* Harrisburg, Penn.: Commonwealth of Pennsylvania, Pennsylvania Historical and Museum Commission, 1972.

Johnston, W., and A. K. *The Scottish Clans and Their Tartans.* Edinburgh: G. W. Bacon, Ltd., 1962.

Martinez, Jimmie, and Arlene Watters, eds. *US: A Cultural Mosaic: A Multicultural Program for Primary Grades.* 823 United Nations Plaza, New York, NY 10017: ADL of B'nai B'rith, n. d.

Quinn, Carin C. "The Jeaning of America—and the World." *American Heritage* 29:3 (April/May 1978):14–21.

Schnurnberger, Lynn. *Let There Be Clothes: 40,000 Years of Fashion.* New York: Workman Publishers, 1991.

UNIT FOUR

THE HIDDEN MEANING OF COLORS

NEW VOCABULARY

gratitude

SUBJECT MATTER

Funeral and mourning customs
Symbolism of colors

ISSUES

▲ Being kind to a stranger
▲ Cultural relativity—not being judgmental about other people's ways
▲ Emotional pain in becoming acculturated
▲ Rewards in learning about other people's traditions

WARM-UP QUESTIONS

▲ What colors does your family wear when they go to weddings and funerals?
▲ Do you know about any cultures in which red, black, or white is worn for special occasions?

The White Headband

Hi. My name is Minh. Cultural differences caused many problems for me when I first came from Vietnam. However, one problem I vividly remember happened during my first week of school between me and my first friend named Angela. She was African American.

It was my fourth or fifth day of school in Texas during the hot summer heat of September. I was sitting at my desk staring around the classroom for I did not understand a word that the teacher was talking about. Suddenly, I noticed that Angela was wearing a white headband. This was the second day I saw her wear it.

In my country, wearing a white headband is a symbol of having a death in the family, especially the death of a parent. By wearing a white headband, the person shows gratitude and gives thanks to the dead person. Wearing it lets others feel sympathy. As for Angela, I was worried for her. She was only ten and had already lost one parent. This was my only concern for her.

Recess came. I walked as fast as I could to Angela. When we both saw each other, she gave me a big smile. With that gesture, I felt funny inside. I told her, "I am sorry," for those were the only few words I could say next to "Hi" and "Thank you."

Angela gave me a weird look and asked, "Why?"

I did not know what to say, so I pointed to her white headband. Angela was confused as to what I was saying, and I was trying my best to tell her. She then asked this Vietnamese guy from another class to ask me what was wrong. I told him the story in my own language. After I was done, he told me

I Felt Like I Was from Another Planet

that it was all right and no one was dying. He spoke with Angela and then left. Angela took off her headband and put it away for she knew what I was trying to tell her.

Now as I think back on the incident I feel embarrassed. If only I knew what the fashion of hairstyles was, I would not have made a fool out of myself. As for Angela and me, we still keep in touch by writing letters.

HEADLINES/OPEN MINDS

Write your answers inside the heads of the characters. You can use words, phrases, or pictures.

1. What do you imagine Angela thought when Minh said, "I'm sorry?"

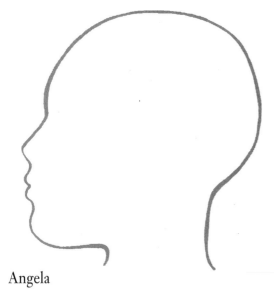

Angela

2. What do you imagine the other Vietnamese student thought when he found out why Minh was concerned?

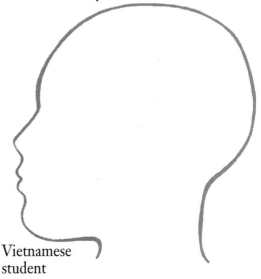

Vietnamese student

3. What do you imagine Angela thought when she found out why Minh was concerned? List at least two thoughts.

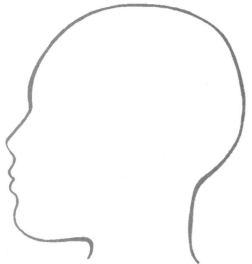

Angela

4. How do you imagine Minh felt when Angela took off her headband?

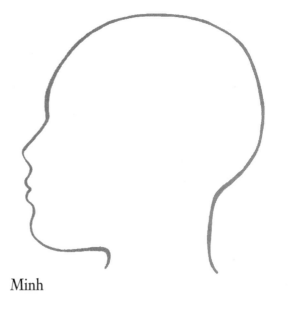

Minh

OPINIONS AND IDEAS

1. What did you expect Angela to do when she found out why Minh was concerned?

2. Were you surprised when Angela took off her headband? Why or why not?

3. What might have happened if Angela had not called over the other Vietnamese student to translate?

4. How would you describe Angela's personality? Would you want her for your friend? Why or why not?

5. Create a different ending for this story.

FOLLOW-UP ACTIVITIES

1. Create a comic strip about "The White Headband." In simple pictures inside boxes show what happened to Minh and Angela. Write balloon dialogue over their heads. If you want, you can even change the ending.

2. Make a list of clothing colors that you and members of your family or culture would never wear on particular occasions or in particular places. List the occasion or place next to each color. If you live in a place where there are gangs, be sure to list colors their members wear that would put you in danger if you wore them.

CULTURAL BACKGROUND

In the U.S. white is the color most associated with a wedding and the bride's dress, but in Asia white is most often the color for funeral clothing. White headbands are worn as a sign of mourning (especially for parents and grandparents). Because of this relationship between death and the color white, an American nurse tells about sick and injured Cambodian refugees who refused to enter an American-run hospital in Thailand because the nurses wore white. In addition, an American manufacturer of appliances ships only almond-colored refrigerators to Hong Kong and Taiwan because these customers believe that white refrigerators will bring death and other bad luck into their households.

In a guidebook for those planning to visit Singapore and Malaysia, tourists are advised not to wear white to a wedding. Instead red, pink, or gold are recommended colors for wedding guests because they are thought to bring good luck. Conversely, red would never be worn to a funeral.

A Chinese American young woman tells how she was dressed in a red summer dress as she drove 500 miles to reach the family home after her grandfather died. As soon as she saw the disappointed look on her relatives' faces, she realized and remembered that her red dress was disrespectful. She had become so Americanized that she had forgotten the family funeral traditions.

Green is another color that has a powerful meaning among some Chinese. A green hat symbolizes an unfaithful wife. At a trade show convention held in Pasadena, California, company representatives who handed out green hats as a promotional giveaway were puzzled when those Chinese in attendance either avoided their booth or took the hats and threw them in the trash. After discovering that the green hat symbolized a cuckolded husband, the booth holders got rid of the hats, substituted coffee mugs as gifts, and became as busy as all the other booths around them.

In contrast, green is a favored color in Muslim cultures. Green is found in the flags of Iraq, Jordan, Saudi Arabia, Pakistan, Lebanon, Syria, Algeria, Morocco, and Egypt. The dome of the famed mosque in Medina is green, and every Arabic dictionary has a green cover.

Colors can be used to make political statements, too. In 1979 when Americans were taken hostage in Iran and later during the 1992 Persian Gulf War, Americans displayed yellow ribbons tied to trees, bridges, utility poles, porch pillars, around ponytails, and pinned to lapels. Yellow ribbons symbolize a nation waiting for its returning warriors, a custom that can be traced as far back as the Civil War.

Funeral and Mourning Customs

In order to maintain their businesses, funeral homes in the United States are having to make adjustments to accommodate the customs of new immigrants. For example, Korean families will not schedule funerals on even-numbered days; Vietnamese immigrants burn incense, necessitating the installation of fans in chapels to draw off the thick smoke; extended families of Asians and Hispanics need larger lying-in-state rooms for prayer vigils. Some cemeteries now provide portable incinerators for those Asian rites requiring the burning of paper money, paper cars, paper homes, and paper furniture. These items are thought to be needed by the deceased in the hereafter.

A few more examples of ethnically individualized customs are given below:

Muslims (who do not believe in embalming) prepare the body themselves using oils and fragrances. Husbands prepare their wives; wives prepare their husbands, and children are prepared by either parent. The eyes and mouth are closed, orifices are packed, and hands and feet are bound. Then the body is shrouded and placed in a casket, which usually remains closed.

Samoan women will dress the body of the deceased, and there is usually a small choir that performs as part of the service. The body is covered with a veil (a tradition growing out of the need to keep off insects in Samoa), and the casket is draped and surrounded with fine mats of handwoven grass or leaves. Before the casket is closed, the spouse or eldest child puts perfume over the body. As the casket is lowered into the ground, mourners throw flowers on it, and the choir sings.

Unlike mourning Vietnamese who wear white headbands, Americans today rarely show their mourning status in public. In the past, men wore black armbands; women dressed in black for a protracted length of time, and families hung black wreaths on doors. Some customs, however, continue to be carried on at home. Some Italian Americans still turn their mirrors to the wall and cover them with black for a week after a funeral. Some American Jews observe this practice as well, and many still observe a seven-day period called *shivah*, during which mourners stay home and suspend work and social activities.

CULTURAL RELATIVITY QUESTIONS

1. In your family, what color dress does the bride wear?

2. In your family, if the bride were dressed in red, what would people say?

3. In your family, if the bride were dressed in black, what would people say?

4. What colors does your family wear to a funeral?

5. In your family, what color clothing might your grandparents object to your wearing? Explain your answer.

6. In your family, what color is considered bad luck? Explain your answer.

7. In your family, are there certain colors of clothing that only boy babies wear and certain colors of clothing that only girl babies wear? Explain your answer.

8. In your family, what would you never wear to a wedding? What would you never wear to a funeral?

9. Are there certain colors that you associate with death in either clothes or flowers?

10. When someone in your family dies, how do you show respect? (Do you stay home from work or school, wear certain clothing or colors, prepare certain foods, say special prayers, light a candle, suspend social activities, and so on?)

LEARNING MORE

The following related topics may be explored: color customs around the world; wedding clothing customs; funeral clothing customs; funeral customs.

TELLING YOUR STORY

Choose one.

▲ Tell about a time when you or someone else wore the wrong color in a certain place or for a certain occasion.

▲ Tell about a time when a pet or a person you loved died.

▲ Tell about a time when someone did something kind and considerate for you.

TELLING YOUR STORY VARIATION

Make a block picture story of any of the above topics. Draw six boxes on a large piece of paper. Draw the pictures in the order that the story happened. Write a few sentences under each picture. Use marking pens, colored pencils, or pen and ink.

TEACHING TIPS

There are three areas of discussion that you can address in this unit, depending on the grade level of the students, the appropriateness of the topics, and your own ease with the subject matter.

▲ Color customs

▲ Death and how humans express sadness at a time of loss over a pet, a friend, a neighbor, or a family member

▲ The kind and unkind ways that students treat one another.

The second Follow-Up Activity shows that students have absorbed color rules but probably have not thought much about them before. Omit the gang color associations if gang activity is not a social reality for your school or if you believe it is inappropriate. On the other hand, if gang activity is of local concern, this might be a nonthreatening way of discussing it.

Cultural sensitivity and relativity are the issues to stress in this unit. Pay tribute to the awareness that Angela had for Minh's predicament and how astute she was to call over a translator in an attempt to understand a confusing moment. When Angela found out the reason for Minh's behavior, Angela's alternatives might have been to shrug her shoulders and walk away or perhaps make an unkind remark about how weird Minh's ideas were. Point out that by Angela's willingness to learn something new she was rewarded with friendship that has lasted for many years.

Ask about new and different customs related to colors, weddings, or funerals that students have learned about on a person-to-person level—from neighbors, classmates, or friends. Evoke enthusiasm for the variety of ways that human beings express emotions—both joy and sorrow—through different customs. Point out that this is always the goal of traveling to other places—seeing something new and different. Suggest that the same opportunity exists at home in a multicultural society if only one is willing to make a move to learn something new.

The Cultural Relativity Questions would make a good interviewing activity. Students could ask the questions of parents or neighbors or friends and report back to the class.

SOURCES

Craig, Jo Ann. *Culture Shock.* No. 1, New Industrial Rd. Off Upper Paya Lobar Rd., Singapore 1953: Times Books International, 1979.

Daniels, Susan. "Funeral Customs of the Newest Americans." *The Director.* (July 1989):10–15.

Dore, Henry, S.J. *Chinese Customs.* Translated by M. Kennelly, S.J. 227 Rangoon Road, Singapore 0821: Graham Brash (Pte) Ltd., 1989.

Malpezzi, Frances M. and William M. Clements. *Italian-American Folklore.* Little Rock, Ark.: August House Publishers, 1992.

Padilla, Steve. "Death's New Face: Funeral Industry Responds to the Immigrant Culture." *Los Angeles Times.* (5 March 1990) B:1, 8.

Sherman, Josepha. *Jewish American Folklore.* Little Rock, Ark.: August House Publishers, 1992.

TABLE MANNERS

NEW VOCABULARY

gourmet

SUBJECT MATTER

Table manners in the U.S. and elsewhere

ISSUES

▲ Cultural adaptations through imitation and trial and error
▲ Cultural relativity—not being judgmental about other people's ways
▲ Influence of cultural rules and customs that have been informally and unconsciously learned and accepted, yet rarely questioned
▲ What is acceptable and approved in one culture can be offensive or unacceptable elsewhere

WARM-UP QUESTIONS

▲ When you sit down for dinner, what rules does your family have?
▲ Have you ever visited someone's home where the rules were different?

Slurping

I realized long before I came to the United States that the Chinese are the best gourmet cooks in the world. I was taught in my native country, Hong Kong, that eating is one of the most enjoyable things to do. We also showed our appreciation to the chef through making noises while enjoying the dish he prepared.

My name is Alex, and when I was attending junior high school, a school organization sponsored a banquet at a formal American restaurant. I was invited as a member of that organization. Everyone was dressed in formal wear, and I was glad I didn't feel out of place because I was wearing a suit. We were shown to our table, and everything went by just fine until they started serving. The soup was first. I held up my spoon and took the first spoonful of soup into my mouth. It was rich clam chowder. I like clam chowder, so I kept pouring soup into my mouth. I enjoyed the soup so much that I almost forgot what was happening. All of a sudden, I experienced a lot of eyeballs staring at me. First I didn't know what happened, but later I realized it was due to the noises I made while drinking the soup. Our organization sponsor came over to ask for the reason of such an action. I explained my culture. I was used to showing my appreciation to the chef by making loud noises. The sponsor explained that such action is not necessary in this country. On the contrary, it was considered rude. The rest of the dinner went by just fine, but I don't remember how the New York steak tasted. I only can remember how hard my heart was beating and how red my face turned.

I Felt Like I Was from Another Planet

I have learned that cultures are different. To avoid feeling out of place, I should watch and learn from others around me. If only I had done so at the restaurant, that embarrassment could have been avoided.

HEADLINES/OPEN MINDS

Write your answers inside the heads of the characters. You can use words, phrases, or pictures.

1. What do you imagine the sponsor thought when he heard Alex making those noises? List at least three thoughts.

2. What do you imagine Alex thought when his sponsor walked over to him?

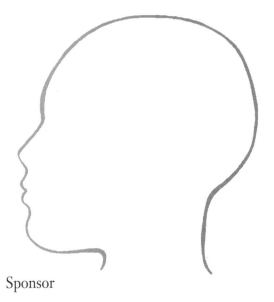

Sponsor

Alex

3. How do you imagine Alex felt after his sponsor returned to his seat?

4. If you had been seated next to Alex, what would you have thought? List at least three thoughts.

Alex

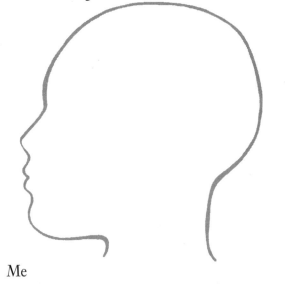

Me

OPINIONS AND IDEAS

1. Should the sponsor have handled the situation differently? Why or why not?

2. Why didn't Alex's classmates tell him to stop slurping?

3. How could Alex's embarrassing situation been avoided?

4. If you had been sitting next to Alex, what would you have done?

5. Alex said that the next time he is in an unfamiliar situation he will look around to see what others are doing first. Do you think this is a good idea? Why or why not?

FOLLOW-UP ACTIVITIES

1. Table Manners Survey: Copy the following list. Ask at least two other students if they are expected to do what is on the list when they eat dinner with their families. Compare your survey numbers with other students' results.

Answer Yes or No to the following.

I can start eating as soon as I sit down.

I have to say a blessing before I eat.

I can read at the table.

I can make noises while eating.

I can belch or burp at the table and no one will scold me.

I can talk with my mouth full.

I have to eat everything on my plate.

I have to eat something even if I don't like it.

I can leave the table without being excused.

I have to stay at the table until everyone is finished.

I have to help clear the table when I am finished.

I have to help with the dishes and cleaning up of the kitchen.

2. Pretend that you work for the United States Visitors Bureau and you want to let newcomers know about our public eating customs in nonethnic restaurants.

Draw one large circle on a piece of paper. Inside the circle illustrate one table rule that is not acceptable in this country, for example, eating rice with fingers. After you finish, draw a diagonal line over it indicating that it is not permitted (as in No Smoking signs, with the line running diagonally over the cigarette). See how many different rules and ways of expressing them you and your classmates can create.

CULTURAL BACKGROUND

In America, making sounds while eating is considered offensive because it is thought to imitate the sounds animals make while eating. Americans are not supposed to slurp liquids or noodles, chew out loud with open mouths, swallow noisily, or sigh with satisfaction after ingesting food. And they are not the only ones to ban sounds. In Malawi (Southeast Africa), children who slurp are also chastised by their parents, who may use a proverb such as, "I hear the guns of the Tyandla people booming," to correct them.

In sharp contrast, in Hong Kong and elsewhere in Asia, making loud sounds pays tribute to the chef. The Vietnamese sometimes smack their lips while eating to show they are enjoying the food. In Saudi Arabia, burping at the table is an acceptable way to show how delicious the food is.

Ideas about table manners have changed through time. Prior to the 16th century, Europeans ate from a common dish and drank from a common goblet. Soups and sauces were commonly drunk by lifting the bowl to the mouth. Nobility threw their gnawed bones back into the common dish, spit on the table and blew their noses into the table cloth. Although forks were introduced as far back as the 11th century, it took eight centuries for them to be accepted, and in some places the fork was banned as being a tool of the devil. Even Martin Luther preached against its use. In 19th century Naples, people ate spaghetti with their hands.

The use of utensils varies throughout the world. Nowadays, in most places in Europe, although the fork, knife, and spoon are used, the fork is generally kept in the left hand while eating and the knife is held in the right hand and used to push food onto the fork. In France even fruit requires a fork and knife. It is first peeled with a knife and then eaten with a fork. In Brazil one cannot use the side of the fork for cutting; only a knife is acceptable. But there is never a knife on the table in China, where, as it was elsewhere in olden times, the knife is considered to be a weapon.

While the fork, knife, and spoon are tools for bringing the food to the mouth, they also provide signals for those who are serving. Where you place them after eating lets others know whether or not you are done. When finished, Spaniards place the knife and fork in parallel positions across the plate. If they are placed on opposite sides of the plate, however, it means, "I would like some more." When Argentineans are finished eating, they cross the knife and fork (with the tines down) in the middle of their plates. In contrast, in Czechoslovakia, a criss-crossed knife and fork on the plate means the diner is only taking a brief rest.

Chopsticks have their own rules. For example, they are never placed upright in rice, for this act is generally considered as an offering to the dead, done only at funerals; it would be unlucky to do so at an ordinary meal. When Asians are finished eating, they place their chopsticks parallel across the dish or bowl. If wooden chopsticks are used it is acceptable to rub them together first to remove the splinters, but this act is thought to be impolite if one is a guest. In addition, guests in China are not supposed to begin eating until the host picks up his or her chopsticks.

In the Middle East where fingers are often used, the food can only be taken with the right hand. (The same is true in other parts of Asia). This is because the left hand is reserved for bodily hygiene. In Morocco it is common to eat with fingers and from a common platter, but again only the right hand is permissible. As an extreme opposite, in Brazil, no fingers may be used to pick up food unless the food is wrapped in a napkin. This rule includes sandwiches and fruit.

There are many eating customs that seem unusual to Americans. Egyptians pour tea into a glass until it overflows onto the saucer. In Portugal, guests show their appreciation for an enjoyable meal by kissing the side of their index finger and then pinching their earlobe between the kissed index finger and the thumb. A variation of this custom exists in Brazil, where satisfied diners will pinch their earlobes between the thumb and forefinger as a sign of pleasure and satisfaction. They will sometimes even reach behind the head and grasp the opposite earlobe to express their content.

What parents haven't admonished their children to "clean your plate!" American children have been advised to do so because others were starving in Europe or China or other places in the news. A Chinese friend told me her mother used to say, "For every grain of rice left on your plate, you will have one pock mark on your face."

Elsewhere cleaning your plate has other meanings. In Bali if you clean your plate it is a sign that you would like more food. In the Philippines diners try to leave a bit of food on the plate to signal that the hosts have provided enough. Similarly in Egypt, diners leave food on the plate as a symbol of abundance and a compliment to the host; in Jordan, leaving a small portion of food on the plate is a sign of politeness.

In ancient times a sacrifice occurred before feasts, and symbolic representations of this custom can still be found. During the sacred Kava ceremony in Samoa, participants hold their cups in front of themselves and spill a few drops on the floor before taking some themselves. Likewise, some Native American tribes may throw tobacco into the fire as an offering while prayers are said; the Igbo people of Nigeria may rotate a pinch of fufu (mashed cassava root) above their heads and throw it outside before eating.

In most parts of the world there are people who give thanks or say grace before or after a meal, especially the evening meal, or at a feast. Arabs will roll back the right sleeve and say *"Bis mil'lah!"* ("In God's name!") before eating and after the meal say *"Hamdallah!"* ("Praise be to God").

Laotians individually say grace after eating by raising clasped hands to the head and thanking God for the meal. In early American rural settings prayers were brief and often humorous,

"Good bread, good meat,

Good God, let's eat!"

or blasphemous,

"Father, Son and Holy Ghost,

Who eats the fastest, gets the most."

Giving thanks for food sometimes takes the form of toasts paying tribute to the food or cook, as in the nonreligious phrases "Bon Appetit!" "Salute!" "Cheers!" "Salud!" "Nostrovya!" "Chin Chin!" "L'Chayim!"

CULTURAL RELATIVITY QUESTIONS

1. In your family, how do you show appreciation to the chef or cook if you have enjoyed a meal that person has prepared?

2. In your family, where do the parents sit?

3. In your family, can children sit in their parents' chairs? What would happen if they did?

4. In your family, who gets served food first? Who gets served last? Who serves the food?

5. What foods are you allowed to eat with your fingers at the dinner table?

6. Do your parents scold you if you waste food? What do they say?

7. In your family, does everyone eat dinner around the table at the same time?

8. In your family, can you watch TV while eating dinner?

9. Does your family say grace or give a blessing before or after the meal? Describe it.

10. Is it customary to thank your mother or father for the meal when you are finished?

LEARNING MORE

The following related topics may be explored: etiquette or table rules in this country; table rules or manners in other countries; history of food utensils.

TELLING YOUR STORY

Choose one.

▲ Tell about a time when you made a mistake in eating rules when dining in a restaurant or at someone else's house.

▲ Tell about a time when someone who had different eating rules visited your home.

▲ Finish this statement: "Alex's story reminds me of the time I . . ."

TELLING YOUR STORY VARIATIONS

Choose one.

▲ Turn any one of the above topics into a filmstrip. On a wide piece of paper, draw a series of pictures of what happened in your story. Draw a box around each picture, making it a picture frame. Pick a partner and tell the story to him or her, pointing out the pictures, frame by frame.

▲ Write a thank-you note to someone who invited you over to share a meal that you enjoyed. Refer to the food and any special parts of the visit that made it memorable.

TEACHING TIPS

Table manners are learned informally and unconsciously, so much so that we take them for granted and assume that others eat in the very same way we do, that is, until we unexpectedly discover that our manners are offensive to others. Alex learned quickly, though painfully, that he was doing something wrong, but figured out a solution for avoiding similar problems the next time. His reaction exemplifies how we all learn to make cultural adaptations.

Toast Alex's method of avoiding future mistakes—that when in an unfamiliar situation he will look around and see what others are doing first before he acts. Emphasize that imitation is the most common and basic form of learning, something we all do consciously and unconsciously. Talk about how customs are absorbed by imitation and reinforced by culture and parents through praise for doing things "right" or scolding for doing things "wrong." Make sure, however, that students don't end up with a sense of "right" and "wrong" table manners from a cross-cultural perspective. Reinforce the concept of cultural relativity. One needs to understand another's different behavior in the context of that person's culture.

The second Follow-Up Activity shows students how much about manners they know even though they might never have articulated these rules before.

Cultural Relativity Questions 2, 3, and 4 ask about where parents and children sit at the table and allude to the issue of authority within the family. This can reveal a lot about family dynamics. You might want to ask the children what they think it means when family members have assigned places that no one else can use.

The various answers to all the Cultural Relativity Questions will demonstrate that what students take for granted as acceptable table behavior may be unacceptable elsewhere.

SOURCES

Axtell, Roger E. *Gestures! Do's and Taboos Around the World*. New York. John Wiley & Sons, 1990.

Farb, Peter, and George Armelagos. *Consuming Passions: The Anthropology of Eating*. Boston: Houghton Mifflin, 1980.

Porter, Kenneth W. "Humor, Blasphemy, and Criticism in the Grace Before Meat." New York: *Folklore Quarterly* 21:1 (February 1965):3–18.

Visser, Margaret. *The Rituals of Dinner*. New York: Grove Weidenfeld, 1991.

UNIT SIX

New Year's and Luck

NEW VOCABULARY

Gung Hay Fat Choy

SUBJECT MATTER

Luck
New Year's customs
Superstitions

ISSUES

▲ Cultural adaptations through imitation and trial and error
▲ Cultural relativity—not being judgmental about other people's ways
▲ Influence of cultural rules and customs that have been informally and unconsciously learned and accepted, yet rarely questioned
▲ Rewards in learning about other people's traditions

WARM-UP QUESTIONS

▲ Is there anything you or your family do at the beginning of the new year to insure that what follows will be a good year?
▲ Is there anything you do or wear to bring good luck or to keep bad luck away?

Gung Hay Fat Choy

I am a second generation Japanese American. My father and mother are first generation Japanese American and they named me Miyumi. When I was in high school I had a boyfriend named Richard who was a first generation Chinese. When we met he had already lived in the United States for seven years. Richard invited me to go to his grandparents' house to celebrate the Chinese New Year. This was a holiday I knew nothing about.

We arrived at his grandparents' home and all of his aunts, uncles, and cousins were there. I expected a lot of people, but I also expected that most of them would speak English. I was surprised when everyone was speaking Chinese. It sounded like they were mad at each other. My boyfriend explained that this was the normal tone of their language.

Everyone was in the den talking to one another while the grandparents greeted all of the younger children, giving red envelopes to each one and saying "Happy New Year" in Chinese. The children happily took their envelopes, which had money inside. The grandparents came to Richard and handed him a red envelope while they said Happy New Year greetings to each other. Next, the grandparents turned to me and gave me a red envelope and I said, "Oh, no. That's OK." The grandparents looked a little puzzled and again tried to hand me the envelope. Richard elbowed me in my side and said, "Take it and say, 'Gung Hay Fat Choy,' which means Happy New Year in Chinese."

By this time all of his relatives' eyes were on me and the room was quiet. I guess everyone wanted to hear me say Happy

I Felt Like I Was from Another Planet

New Year in Chinese. My palms were all sweaty and I was feeling really nervous. I thought to myself, I wish I hadn't come.

I turned to Richard and said, "What do I say again?" He repeated, "Gung Hay Fat Choy" so I turned to his grandparents and said, "Gung Hay Fat Choy" the best way I knew how. At that instant the whole room broke out in laughter and the grandparents handed me the envelope and smiled. Even though I was extremely embarrassed, I was very relieved. I asked my boyfriend if I had insulted his grandparents, and he said, "No, you did good."

After this embarrassing scene, Richard's mother came to me and said in her broken English, "You talk Chinese good," and we both exchanged smiles.

HEADLINES/OPEN MINDS

Write your answers inside the heads of the characters. You can use words, phrases, or pictures.

1. What do you imagine Richard's grandparents thought when Miyumi refused to take the red envelope? List at least two thoughts.

2. How do you imagine Richard felt when Miyumi refused to take the red envelope?

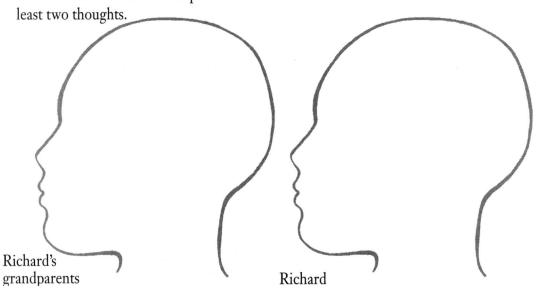

Richard's grandparents

Richard

3. How do you imagine Miyumi felt when Richard insisted that she take the envelope and talk in Chinese?

4. How do you imagine Richard's mother felt when Miyumi finally said "Gung Hay Fat Choy" and took the envelope? List at least two feelings.

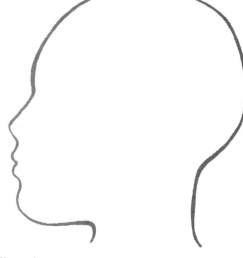

Miyumi

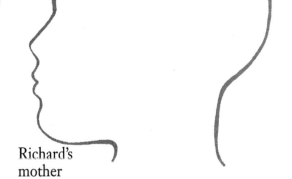

Richard's mother

OPINIONS AND IDEAS

1. Why did Miyumi think Richard's relatives were mad at each other?

2. On New Year's what could be the meaning of giving a red envelope with money inside?

3. If you had been Miyumi, would you have been able to speak in Chinese to Richard's grandparents? Why or why not?

4. Should Richard have warned Miyumi ahead of time about what to expect? Why or why not?

5. Do you think Richard's family was upset that he brought a non-Chinese person to this family gathering? Why or why not?

FOLLOW-UP ACTIVITIES

1. Pick a partner and make red envelopes to exchange, but instead of putting money inside, put in a wish for something good to happen to that person (you will soon take a vacation; you will get all A's; you will be chosen for the baseball team; and so on) or a compliment (you have the most beautiful hair; you are a very kind person; you are fun to be with; and so on). Write your wish or compliment on a small piece of paper.

To make the envelope, cut red tissue paper or red wrapping paper into 6-inch squares. Place the message in the center of the red square. Fold all corners to the center, slightly overlapping them. Use a gold sticker to hold the corners together. A notary seal works well. If gold pens are available, decorate the envelopes with designs.

2. Make a Chinese lunar calendar. Draw a large circle on a big piece of paper. If you do this at home, use a dinner plate to draw around. If you do it at school, use a compass or tie one end of a string around a pencil and attach the other end of the string to the center of your paper to draw the circle.

Divide the circle into 12 sections by drawing with a ruler. First divide the circle into half, then half again, and continue until you have 12 pie-shaped pieces.

Each pie-shaped piece represents a different animal symbol. Draw the animal inside the pie shape. The order of the animal symbols is as follows, going clockwise around the circle: Dragon, Snake, Horse, Sheep, Monkey, Rooster, Dog, Boar, Rat, Ox, Tiger, Rabbit.

At the bottom of the page, write your name and the year in which you were born. Example: My name is Zachary and I was born in the Year of the Dragon.

The Chinese believe that the year in which you were born and the representative animal named for it affects your personality. Under your name and year, describe at least one way in which your personality is like the animal symbol. Example: My name is Zachary and I was born in the Year of the Dragon. That is why I am strong and powerful and people are sometimes afraid of me.

Here is the cycle of years and the animals they correspond with.

Dragon (1952, 1964, 1976, 1988)   Snake (1953, 1965, 1977, 1989)

Horse (1954, 1966, 1978, 1990)   Sheep (1955, 1967, 1979, 1991)

Monkey (1956, 1968, 1980, 1992)   Rooster (1957, 1969, 1981, 1993)

Dog (1958, 1970, 1982, 1994)   Boar (1959, 1971, 1983, 1995)

Rat (1960, 1972, 1984, 1996)   Ox (1961, 1973, 1985, 1997)

Tiger (1962, 1974, 1986, 1998)   Rabbit (1951, 1963, 1975, 1987)

CULTURAL BACKGROUND

Red envelopes are called *lai see*. In Chinese tradition, married adults give them to children and single adults on Chinese New Year. Envelopes with money are given on other symbolic occasions as well, such as to a doctor before surgery or the birth of a child; at a wedding banquet; for congratulations, gratitude, or compensation. In contrast, white envelopes with money are given for funerals.

The *lai see* are red with gold decorations and both colors are considered lucky colors in Chinese tradition. The envelopes are usually decorated with gold good-wish designs, which are like greeting cards in the messages they convey.

Depending on the Chinese lunar calendar, Chinese New Year takes place sometime between mid-January to mid-February. Other Chinese New Year's customs include the setting off of firecrackers, wearing new clothes, elaborate feasting, thorough housecleaning before the new year, red good-luck banners hanging in the home. Children must be extra well-behaved; sharp-edged instruments and tools (needles, knives, etc.) are put away; flowers, burning incense, and other offerings to ancestors are placed on family altars.

In the Chinese lunar calendar each year is named after an animal. This is based on the belief that when Buddha summoned all living creatures to him, only 12 came. In tribute to these faithful, he named a year after each one in the order of their arrival, beginning with the Rat.

The carrying out of New Year's rituals is a testimony to the human spirit. It demonstrates that people everywhere have faith in the future—in the continuance of life. Regardless of the group of people or when the new year falls on different calendars, principles for celebrating the New Year are similar.

In all cultures, the New Year is a time to clean the slate of the past year and start anew with anticipation and optimism. For most people, how you begin the new year determines what the rest of the year will be like. What you do on New Year's Day you will do all year long. Consider then, the terror of the newly arrived Chinese family who found a mortuary ad in their mailbox on Chinese New Year.

To ensure that only good things will happen, people commonly eat foods representing wealth (black-eyed peas for African Americans). Elsewhere, people make certain that only approved persons will ever cross the threshold, keeping the home safe. This explains the custom of the "first foot" as practiced in Scotland, where people arrange for a dark-haired man to be the first one to cross the threshold right after midnight on New Year's Eve.

The Japanese celebrate their New Year (Oshogatsu) on January 1. At midnight on December 31, temple bells ring 108 times to drive away the 108 ego attachments of human beings. A *mochi* (rice cake) soup cooked with vegetables and other food is eaten by most Japanese as the first meal of the new year, ensuring a happy new year to come. On New Year's Day two archers each send one arrow into the air to clear it of evil spirits. New Year celebrants also play *hanetsuki*, a game like shuttlecock and battledore, in which elaborately decorated paddles are used to hit small feathered, wooden balls.

In Italy, people eat lentils with pork on New Year's Eve, believing that each lentil will equal the amount of money earned in the new year. Wearing red brings good luck, and so does eating lobster. On New Year's Eve at midnight, Italians are supposed to throw anything old out the window and onto the street—plates, furniture, and so on. Especially in Southern

Italy, it is dangerous to be in the streets at midnight when items are being tossed out.

Vietnamese New Year, called Tet, is similar to the Chinese celebration. Cars are washed, houses are repainted, and furniture is cleaned ahead of time. Children and adults wear new clothes. No household rubbish is thrown away during the first three days of the year. Children are not allowed to cry, because that would mean crying for the rest of the year. Similarly, scolding children is forbidden. Tet is also considered the wedding season. People choose this time to get married because they believe the happiness of their first days of being married will stay with them for the rest of the year and the rest of their lives.

Depending on the lunar calendar, the Jewish New Year (*Rosh Hashanah*) takes place in mid or late September. It resembles other New Year celebrations as a time to wear new clothing, but it is a more somber, reflective occasion, with most of it taking place in the temple. This is the time for a spiritual inventory. The primary feature is to pray for a renewal of life, to ask that sins be pardoned and that one's life be filled with health, blessings, and prosperity. Ten days following is *Yom Kippur*, the Day of Atonement, marked by fasting and more prayer.

Iranians celebrate their New Year in the spring and call the event *Nou-Rooz*. At home the New Year's table is set with seven traditional items beginning with the letter *S* (called *haft seen* in Farsi): *serkeh* (vinegar), *seeb* (apple), *sekkeh* (gold coin) or *seam* (silver coin), *sonbol* (beautiful flower), *sear* (garlic), *sumac* (dried crushed tart berries), and *samanoo* (a sweet pudding of wheat). Other traditional items set out are a bowl of goldfish, the Koran, pomegranates, and pictures of relatives. At this time Iranians eat a special soup of noodles, mint, garlic, and vinegar. On the 13th day of the new year it is considered bad luck to stay indoors, so Iranians must go outdoors with their families to a picnic-like event and watch an ancient sport called the dance of the *hereos varzesh baustani*. Here men and boys dressed in colorful embroidered knickers dance in a circle, juggling 40-pound pins and chanting words of an ancient epic to a drum accompaniment.

Special features of each of these New Year celebrations consist of performing certain acts that will bring good luck or avoiding certain acts to prevent bad luck from striking. These ritual acts (sometimes disparagingly called superstitions) are performed whether one believes in them or not. This occurs everywhere and is not limited to New Year's. For example, people all over the world wear amulets or display them in their homes to keep them from harm. In the Middle East, among both Moslems and Jews, the symbol of a hand with outstretched fingers protects from the evil eye. Asians wear jade for protection; Catholics wear crosses for the same purpose, and in Italy the sign of the horn (*cornu*) offers the same safety.

Numbers, too, have lucky and unlucky characteristics. For example, in the U.S., the most common idea is that 13 is an unlucky number. For this reason most tall buildings do not have a 13th floor; there is no row 13 on some airliners; some airports have no Gate 13; and surgeons and patients are reluctant to have operations scheduled for Friday the 13th. Similarly in China, the word for the number four sounds like the word for death. For this reason Chinese people will avoid addresses with the number four, and hotels often eliminate the fourth floor. Some airports in Asia have no Gate Four.

Numbers can have positive attributes as well. For Jews, each letter of the Hebrew alphabet has an equivalent number. The word *chai* (meaning "life," as in the expression *L'chayim*, a common toast meaning "to life"), is made up of two letters that add up to the number 18. As a result, oberservant Jews will give money to charity in amounts that are multiples of 18 to honor a child's birth, for a *bar mitzvah*, for a graduation, or in thanks for a relative's recovery from illness.

The number three is considered the most popular number in the U.S. Anthropologists call favored numbers "numerical native categories." These numbers are not universal. Most Native American people have the number four as the favored number, while five is the favored number in most of South America and China.

CULTURAL RELATIVITY QUESTIONS

1. On what date does your family celebrate New Year's?

2. What do you call New Year's?

3. How do you say "Happy New Year" in another language?

4. What kinds of things does your family do to prepare for the New Year?

5. Outside of New Year's, what are some things you do or say to keep bad luck from happening to you?

6. What kind of good luck charm do you wear?

7. What do you consider your lucky number?

8. What do you consider your lucky color?

9. Do you have a piece of clothing you wear that seems to bring good luck? When do you wear it?

10. Do you have an object in your home to protect the family from ill health or bad luck? Explain your answer.

LEARNING MORE

The following related topics may be explored: New Year's celebrations of different ethnic groups; good luck; bad luck; superstitions, amulets, omens.

TELLING YOUR STORY

Choose one.

▲ Tell how your family celebrates the New Year.

▲ Tell about a time when you had either very good luck or very bad luck.

TELLING YOUR STORY VARIATION

Choose one.

▲ Make an advertisement for a good luck charm that you think works well. Draw the object and then write phrases or sentences that describe what the object will do for the person who wears or carries it. You can use regular pen, colored marking pens or crayons, or a combination of these media.

▲ Draw a picture of one of your favorite New Year's celebrations. Check to see if the following ritual items are included: flowers, fire, gifts, music, special clothing, special foods, fun.

TEACHING TIPS

New Year's is a time of new beginnings, and people everywhere celebrate it in some unique way, yet there are more similarities than differences in the features of the different celebrations. Through these celebrations humans demonstrate their faith in life and optimism about the future by performing acts to ensure good fortune, good health, and happiness. Discussing the variety of New Year's rituals is a simple way to show that different ethnic groups are more similar than different.

If you choose to do the second Follow-Up Activity, tie in the relationship of the Chinese lunar calendar with the signs of the zodiac. See which animals are used for both. What symbols are unique to each one? Discuss how both of these systems are used to explain why differences occur between people's personalities and success in life. You might ask students if they know their own astrological sign, if they ever read their horoscope, or if their parents do. Not only at New Year's but throughout the year, people are concerned about their future well-being. The zodiac and Chinese lunar calendar attest to humans' ancient concern about survival.

Actions that we take to bring good luck or prevent bad luck will stimulate a lively classroom discussion. However, be sure to watch that students are not put down for any unusual beliefs or customs they might have. The information about the number 13 has been included to remind students that almost everybody has some beliefs in luck, bad or good. Remind students that many athletes wear "lucky clothing," such as certain socks for important games. Convey the concept that the word *superstition* has a negative connotation—that one person's superstition is another person's belief.

Some of the Cultural Relativity Questions might be good ones for students to use to interview neighbors, family friends, or classmates in other rooms. This will enlarge the data base for a spirited discussion.

Miyumi was apprehensive about speaking in another language and participating in a new custom, a New Year's custom that was different and unusual. Point out that this is a normal response, and it took courage on Miyumi's part to try to overcome her fear of making a mistake. We all have the same apprehensions. However, it appears that Miyumi's desire to please Richard and his grandparents was stronger than her fear of trying something new. She is to be given credit for her decision and for taking a step toward understanding someone different from herself.

SOURCES

Allen, Judy, Earldene McNeill, and Velma Schmidt. *Cultural Awareness for Children.* Menlo Park, Calif.: Addison Wesley, 1992.

The California Collection. UCLA Archive of Popular Beliefs and Superstitions. University of California, Los Angeles.

Cuniberti, Betty. "With a Little Luck, You'll Survive Friday the 13th." *Los Angeles Times* (13 March 1987):V:1,4.

Dundes, Alan. "The Number Three in American Culture." *Every Man His Way: Readings in Cultural Anthropology.* Englewood Cliffs, N.J.: Prentice Hall, 1968.

Eberly, Peter. "'Trademarks' of the Chinese (I)". 14Fl. No. 17, Hsuchang St., Taipei 100, Taiwan, Republic of China: *Sinorama Magazine*, 1992.

Martinez, Jimmie, and Arlene Watters, eds. *US: A Cultural Mosaic: A Multicultural Program for Primary Grades.* 823 United Nations Plaza, New York, NY 10017: ADL of B'nai B'rith, n.d.

Newman, Maria. "Happy Nou-Rooz: Iranians Celebrate New Year and Keep Their Customs Alive." *Los Angeles Times* (1 March 1991):A:3.

Oshogatsu. 244 South San Pedro Street, Los Angeles, CA 90012: Japanese American Cultural and Community Center, 1982.

Peng, Tan Huay. *Fun with Chinese Festivals.* P.O. Box 1013, Union City, CA 94587. Heian International, 1991.

Rosten, Leo. *The Joys of Yiddish.* New York: Pocket Books, 1968.

"The Year of the Ram: Chinatown Rings in the New Year." *Angeles* (February 1991):92–99.

PHYSICAL CONTACT

NEW VOCABULARY

flirt

SUBJECT MATTER

Greeting customs

Taboo touching in our culture

Taboo touching in other cultures

ISSUES

▲ Being caught between parents' old world customs and American customs and values

▲ Emotional pain in becoming acculturated

▲ What is accepted and approved in one culture can be offensive or unacceptable elsewhere

WARM-UP QUESTIONS

▲ Have you ever had to do something against your parents' rules?

▲ Have you ever expected your parents to be angry with you about something you did, but they acted in a surprising way?

My name is Amy. I was born in Vietnam. I was taught Chinese culture there. My parents always reminded me not to hold hands or have contact with the opposite sex. Girls were to behave properly and not flirt with boys. However, when I started in the fourth grade in this country, I had to make a decision. Chinese or American cultures? That is when we had square dancing at school and our partners were of the opposite sex.

Cinco de Mayo was the day that all fourth graders performed a Mexican square dance for the whole school. At first I didn't understand what was going on because every student was so excited about this event. Our first rehearsal shocked me. All my classmates knew what to do and had already chosen their partners. I was afraid even to stand close to Billy, the partner my teacher, Mrs. Garey, had chosen for me.

When the music began, Mrs. Garey showed us the steps of the dance. We were supposed to hold hands, twist and turn with our partners. Billy tried to grab hold of my hand when the music started, but I moved away. While everyone else enjoyed the dance, Billy and I stood one foot apart and didn't even move. It was weird that he didn't switch partners on me. The teacher saw that we weren't moving so she asked, "Why are you not dancing?"

Neither of us replied. Mrs. Garey was nice at first and thought that we didn't understand the steps, so she showed them to us again, but the whole afternoon Billy and I just stood there. I turned red. After class Mrs. Garey talked to us and I felt the heat in her throat. She ordered us to dance the next day.

I Felt Like I Was from Another Planet

The next morning I was so afraid to attend class but I had no way to escape. As I watched each second on the clock go by, my heart beat harder. Soon our rehearsal started again. This time Billy urged me to do what I was told, but I was still afraid to go against my parents' rule. As the music began everyone danced, but I just stood there again. Billy tried to hold my hand but every time he did, I stepped back. He got so impatient he pushed me down to the floor, and I began to cry. Mrs. Garey became angry and told me to stand in the corner. While everyone else was having fun, I was suffering from embarrassment.

After class she yelled at me and asked, "Why didn't you dance?" I was crying so hard that I couldn't reply, but I promised her that I would dance the next day. She gave me a smile and handed me a costume, a Mexican dress I was to wear on the day of the performance.

When I got home I hid the costume. Nobody knew about it. I planned to go against my parents' rule because in order to stay in school I knew I had better obey my teacher's order. After all, my parents wouldn't be there when I performed.

The next day I participated with all the students. My classmates were surprised and gave me a welcoming smile. It was my first time to hold a boy's hand and it felt warm. Since I was a fast learner I had no problem catching up. Billy was generous and corrected my mistakes. We both had fun throughout the whole rehearsal.

The performance began and I was so nervous when the principal announced that the fourth graders were going to dance. The music began and even though we were in stiff costumes we danced exactly like the teacher wanted. We paid close attention and knew we danced perfectly because the parents and staff clapped loudly. After we finished, Mrs. Garey acted so proud of us.

What shocked me the most was that my parents were there watching. They caught sight of me, came over, and smiled. They said, "You dance very well!" I was surprised because I thought they would slap me or something. Instead, they accepted what I had done. Later I understood that my whole family had begun to accept American culture.

HEADLINES/OPEN MINDS

Write your answers inside the heads of the characters. You can use words, phrases, or pictures.

1. How do you imagine Amy felt when Billy tried to hold her hand? List at least two feelings.

2. What do you imagine Billy thought when Amy wouldn't hold his hand?

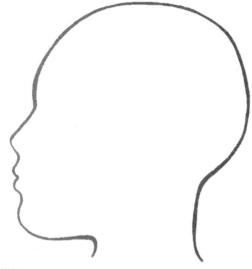

Amy

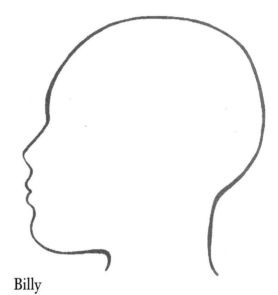

Billy

3. What do you imagine Amy was thinking while she was dancing (before she knew her parents were watching)?

4. How do you imagine Amy felt after she discovered that her parents saw her dance with Billy?

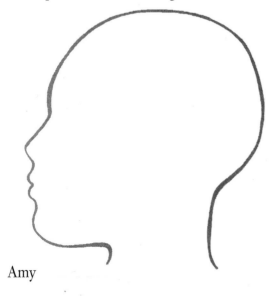

Amy

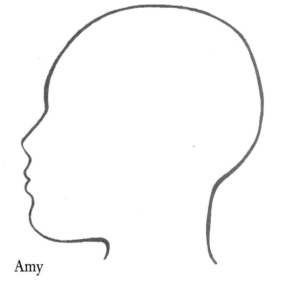

Amy

OPINIONS AND IDEAS

1. Should Amy have explained Chinese customs to her teacher? Why or why not?

2. What would the teacher have done if Amy had told her why she was afraid to hold Billy's hand?

3. Why did Billy push Amy to the floor? What other action could he have taken instead?

4. Do you know of any other families who have similar rules about boys not holding hands with girls? Explain your answer.

5. What customs outside your home have been difficult for your parents to accept?

FOLLOW-UP ACTIVITIES

1. Retell the story from Billy's point of view. This can be done in written or oral form.

2. At recess or lunchtime or after school observe some of the touching behavior of your classmates and friends. When they are walking and talking how much body contact do they have? Do boys touch one another more often than girls do? Do girls have a softer touch? Do boys push each other more? What kinds of similarities and differences can you see between boys and girls and between different ethnic groups?

CULTURAL BACKGROUND

Throughout Asia members of the opposite sex have commonly been taught to avoid touching each other in public. Even if they are married they do not touch or display affection. Specifically, among Laotians a woman who holds the hand of a man is considered daring, and it is insulting to a woman if a man touches her in public. If she allows it then she is considered an "easy" woman.

In contrast, same-sex physical contact is acceptable. Therefore, in Asian and Middle Eastern countries it is common to see males walking hand in hand or with linked arms and females walking together holding hands. This custom often causes problems when immigrants from these countries move to the U.S. Over here when girls walk together holding hands or men link arms they may be perceived as being homosexuals, which may cause confusion and embarrassment.

Rules about acceptable and nonacceptable body contact extend to greeting forms as well. Shaking hands is not very common in most Asian cultures, especially Japan. A more widely accepted greeting seems to be a slight nod of the head toward the person just met. One should avoid extending one's hand to a Vietnamese woman, unless she initiates such action. In places such as Saudi Arabia or Thailand, touching a woman, even in a handshake, is unacceptable.

Conversely, American businessmen in Europe and South America are advised to shake hands with all persons present every time they encounter them even if they are close acquaintances and have already shaken their hands that day. Similarly, in Kenya a man and wife who eat breakfast together and then see each other only a few hours later will shake hands. According to experts, Belgians are thought to be the busiest handshakers among Europeans, while the French are the most reticent. In China the pumping handshake shows pleasure in the greeting.

Americans expect a firm, solid grip when they shake hands. Anything less is sometimes interpreted as untrustworthy and unfriendly. Among Middle Easterners and Asians, however, a firm handclasp suggests aggressiveness, so their handshake is more gentle. Likewise in France, a strong pumping handshake is considered uncultured. It should be brisk and quick.

In Saudi Arabia when two men meet they say, *"Salaam alaykum"* ("Peace be with you"), shake hands and say, *"Kaif halak"* ("How are you?"). One Saudi will extend his left hand to the other's right shoulder and kiss him on both cheeks and perhaps take the other man's hand in his. Americans often want to pull away their hands from an Arab handshake because it lasts too long. Pulling away is offensive to Arabs.

An unusual form of handshake occurs in some parts of Germany. When people arrive at a large dinner table and it is awkward to reach across and shake hands, they will rap their knuckles lightly on the table as a form of greeting and may repeat the gesture when they leave. University students also rap their knuckles on desks when greeting their professors.

More handshaking variations exist. Ghanaian and Nigerian men have complex handslapping greetings. No doubt these West African practices are related to the African American "high five" (slapping hands high in the air), "low five" (slapping hands low in the air), and variations as seen among athletes and used by young people of any ethnicity. This custom is an outgrowth of earlier handslapping practices popular among African American musicians: "Give me five," a request for a quick hand slap, and its 1930s antecedent, "Give me some skin," where palms meet and pull back in a slow sliding motion.

In Latin countries including Italy, Spain, and Sicily, the *abrazo* (hug) is common between men and men, women and women. It is often accompanied by pats on the back. In Mexico, in addition to the *abrazo* the handshake is also used, but in some regions after gripping the palm the two people slide their hands upward and grasp each other's thumbs.

Bowing is the traditional form of greeting in Japan. The Japanese prefer no body contact, although businessmen interacting with their American and European counterparts have accommodated to the handshaking tradition. Bowing requires that the hands slide down toward the knees or remain at the side. The back and neck are held in a stiff position while the eyes look downward. The person in the inferior position always bows lower and longer.

In India, Sri Lanka, and Bangladesh the *namaste* is the preferred form of greeting for both hello and goodbye. Hands are held chest-high in a prayer-like position accompanied by a slight bow forward. Thailand has a comparable gesture called the *wai*, meaning hello, thank you, goodbye, and I'm sorry.

Women in Europe and in Latin America use a social kiss for greetings. In some countries they kiss once, but they actually only brush each other's cheeks and make the kissing sound. In other places, they alternate cheeks, as in France; in Belgium they may kiss three times, alternating cheeks. In Brazil, married women kiss each other on both cheeks, but if one or the other person is unmarried, a third kiss is added, meaning a wish for marriage for the single woman.

CULTURAL RELATIVITY QUESTIONS

1. Would your parents object to your holding hands with someone of the opposite sex while square dancing?

2. Would your parents object to your holding hands with someone of the opposite sex if you were not dancing and you both were ten years old?

3. At what age would it be acceptable for you to hold hands with someone of the opposite sex?

4. Have you ever felt uncomfortable when your parents expected you to greet someone you had never met before by giving them a kiss or a hug?

5. When your family members greet one another do they shake hands, hug and kiss, bow, or do something else?

6. How do your family members usually greet friends? Do women greeting women hug, shake hands, or kiss, or do something else? Do men greeting men hug, shake hands, kiss, or do something else?

7. In your family, when good friends or family members greet each other with a kiss, do they kiss on one cheek, two cheeks, or do they kiss three times? Do they alternate cheeks?

8. When you come to school each morning, is it customary to kiss your parents goodbye?

9. In your family, how do children say good night to parents? Do they hug, kiss, use words, or do something else?

10. In your family, is it acceptable for husbands and wives to kiss or hug in front of the children?

LEARNING MORE

The following related topics may be explored: greeting customs; body language; gestures.

TELLING YOUR STORY

Choose one.

▲ Tell about a time when you had to break your parents' rules.

▲ Tell about a time when you expected your parents to be angry with you about something you did, but they were not.

▲ Tell about a time when your parents had a difficult time accepting customs or some behavior of your friends or classmates.

▲ Tell about a time when you were expected to greet someone in a way that was uncomfortable for you.

TELLING YOUR STORY VARIATIONS

Choose one.

▲ Pick a partner and role play. One of you is the parent and the other is the child. Have the parent scold the child for breaking a particular rule. Have the child defend himself or herself. The parent can either stay angry about the situation or act in a surprising way. Perform your play for the other students.

▲ Divide a piece of paper into two parts. Label one side Greeting Family Members. Label the other side Greeting Friends. On one side illustrate how your family members greet one another. Label each person and their role in the family. On the other side illustrate how your family members greet a friend. You may show kissing, handshaking, bowing, nodding, waving, or something else.

TEACHING TIPS

This unit is significant because it reveals how students' school rules may conflict with home (cultural) rules and how stressful this may be for children, particularly if they feel they cannot discuss the situation with either the teacher or their parents. Since most children want to please their parents and win their approval, it is exceedingly difficult for them when they are in a situation where they must go against parental rules. The sad part is that most teachers would be helpful and might be able to alleviate the students' stress if only they were more aware.

Amy's decision was painful for her to make, yet her story had a happy ending. That is not always so. You have the opportunity to explore this issue in the first Warm-Up Question.

Talk about Billy's behavior. Since he did not have information about why Amy didn't hold his hand, he probably imagined many reasons; for example, "She doesn't like me." Talk about how common this is. We misread a person's reaction and somehow think we are implicated. Yet Amy's response had nothing to do with Billy on a personal level. Use Headline 2 to develop this concept.

The first Follow-Up Activity heightens students' awareness of differing perspectives on a situation. It shows how lack of information can give a distorted view of reality that can potentially be harmful. It is also a useful writing device.

Regarding Cultural Relativity Questions 8 and 9, emphasize that just because a parent does not kiss a child or vice-versa does not mean that parents and children don't love one another. This would only be an outsider's perspective. Parents and children may express love in other ways approved by their culture. Here is another opportunity to talk about making wrong assumptions because of missing cultural information.

If you elect to do the first Telling Your Story Variation, it might be useful to videotape the role playing.

SOURCES

Armour, Monica, Paula Knudson, and Jeffrey Meeks, eds. *The Indochinese: New Americans.* Provo, Utah: 1981.

Axtell, Roger E. *Gestures! The Do's and Taboos of Body Language Around the World.* New York: John Wiley and Sons, 1991.

Copeland, Lennie, and Lewis Griggs. *Going International: How to Make Friends and Deal Effectively in the Global Marketplace.* New York: Plume, 1986.

UNIT EIGHT

RITES OF PASSAGE

NEW VOCABULARY
- abnormal
- gawking
- violation

SUBJECT MATTER
- Different laws and rules in different countries
- Driving rules
- Rites of passage
- Significance of the car in this society
- What it means to be an adult

ISSUES
- ▲ Cultural relativity—not being judgmental about other people's ways
- ▲ What is accepted and approved in one culture can be offensive or unacceptable elsewhere

WARM-UP QUESTIONS
- ▲ Do you know anybody who has ever received a traffic ticket? What for? What happened?
- ▲ At what age do you become an adult?

Hi. I'm Carmen and when I was ten years old I learned to drive a car. In Mexico, this is very common among kids. Some even learn to drive when they're nine years old. For me, it took a while but I learned.

One day, a week after I arrived in the United States, I was very tempted to check out the school where I was supposed to attend, so I got my aunt's car and drove around the school. Everything seemed normal until school was almost over and a crowd of anxious parents began to gather around the main entrance and began staring at me.

At first I ignored them, but soon their gawking disturbed me. Thus, I decided to park the car to see if their abnormal behavior would go away. Since it was a time when most of the parking spaces were full, it was hard for me to find one. Suddenly, I saw this van leaving that was parked on the opposite side of the street. I said to myself, "This has to be mine!"

Right when the van took off I parked my car, but what I didn't know was that a cop was right in back of me and that I just couldn't park facing the cars that were parked on the opposite curb. Since this was not a traffic violation in Mexico, I thought I was doing right. Well, I got a big ticket— for parking absolutely inappropriately, for being under age, for not having a seat belt on, and for not having a license. The worst part of this incident was that almost all the students were watching me, and I knew that I was not going to be able to hang around with them because they were going to make fun of me.

I Felt Like I Was from Another Planet

When I got home with the cops my aunt and my mother were waiting for me with mad-looking faces. I certainly knew I was going to get it and good, but after giving me a lesson, my mother was very understanding. I told her that if I had only known the American traffic rules, this wouldn't have happened.

After this embarrassing incident I studied the driving booklet very hard and until this time I have never gotten one more ticket. The good part of this incident was that the students who had seen me were my friends after all and even admired me for knowing how to drive a vehicle at such a young age.

HEADLINES/OPEN MINDS

Write your answers inside the heads of the characters. You can use words, phrases, or pictures.

1. What do you imagine parents were thinking as they watched Carmen drive around the school? List at least four thoughts.

2. What do you imagine the schoolkids were thinking as they watched Carmen drive? List at least three thoughts.

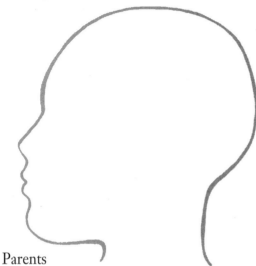

Parents

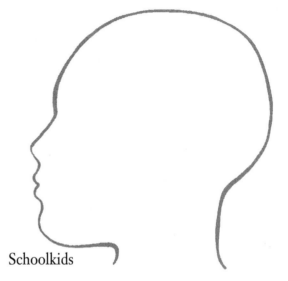

Schoolkids

3. What do you imagine the policeman thought when he saw Carmen driving and parking?

4. What do you imagine Carmen's mother thought when she saw the policeman bringing Carmen home? List at least three thoughts.

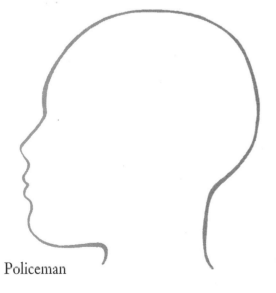

Policeman

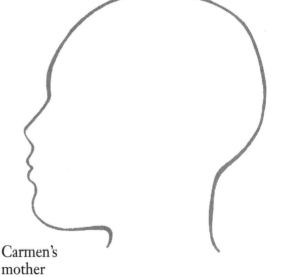

Carmen's mother

OPINIONS AND IDEAS

1. Who called the police? Why do you think so?

2. Should the policeman have given Carmen a ticket? Why or why not?

3. Should Carmen have been punished? Why or why not?

4. Did you expect that Carmen would become a hero to her classmates? Why or why not?

5. Was what Carmen did foolish or dangerous or something else? Explain your answer.

FOLLOW-UP ACTIVITIES

1. Pretend you are a TV or a radio news reporter and you have been called to cover the story of Carmen's driving adventure. You are at the school when the police arrive. Give an eyewitness report to your audience. You may also want to interview a parent, the police, a student, or Carmen. Use a lively style of reporting details.

2. If you worked for the Department of Motor Vehicles, what rules would you have for drivers? Make a list of requirements regarding the following questions:

▲ At what age should a person be allowed to drive alone?

▲ What kind of training should a person have? (behind the wheel, learning rules and regulations)

▲ What kind of health restrictions should there be?

▲ Who should be prevented from driving?

▲ How often should a driver's license be renewed?

▲ At what age should a person no longer be allowed to drive?

▲ If someone breaks a driving rule and another person gets hurt as a result, what should happen to the driver who caused the accident?

▲ If drivers have been drinking, what should happen to them?

Compare your answers to the driving regulations of your state.

CULTURAL BACKGROUND

The popularity of having personalized license plates, deluxe sound systems, cellular phones, and fax machines installed in automobiles reveals that the car in America is more than just a means of transportation. In cities such as Los Angeles, there is even a celebration called The Blessing of the Car held as a way to honor the relationship between the car and the family.

The car is an important symbol of independence, status, and individuality. That is why Carmen became a kind of hero for her new American classmates. She unexpectedly ensured her popularity by showing off her mastery of the automobile. The car is so important that anyone who can control it through driving and parking skills is looked upon favorably, and if that someone is only a child, then she or he is treated with awe.

In Mexico, as in many other parts of the world, there is little difficulty in obtaining a driver's license as long as one has a car and can afford to purchase a license. There is no driving test required, either. Although the laws differ from state to state, most U.S. driving laws are quite strict. For example, most states require the use of seat belts, and drivers must be insured in case of accidents.

Obtaining one's driver's license is an important event, especially in areas where residents are dependent upon cars, because they must travel great distances on a daily basis. In California, the sixteenth birthday marks the date when a teenager can legally drive alone. Most 16-year-olds spend this birthday at the Department of Motor Vehicles eagerly waiting to take the test for their license; parents may begin worrying about insurance costs and liability.

The act of obtaining a driver's license can be interpreted as a rite of passage—a ritual marking the transition from childhood to adulthood. Rites of passage are rituals that cluster at important moments in an individual's life. They are found in every culture worldwide. The most common ones center around birth, entry into adulthood (often called rites of initiation or puberty), marriage, and death.

Cross-cultural rituals celebrating the symbolic move from childhood into adulthood abound, and while the American ritual of obtaining the driver's license usually only involves one parent and the 16-year-old, most ethnic rites of initiation have large numbers of witnesses celebrating the event with music, gifts, special foods, flowers, and joyousness and a sense of community.

For Mexican females, the *quinceañera* (celebration for a 15-year-old girl) marks an occasion that is connected to the Aztec belief that a woman does not become a human being until she is 15. The event is almost as elaborate as a wedding. The celebrant is dressed in a bridelike gown and walks into the church where she is accompanied by formally attired female attendants and their escorts, sometimes as many as 14 couples. Mass is said, there is a renewal of baptismal vows, and the young woman says a prayer to the Virgin Mary. After the church ceremony, the young woman celebrates at a party where she makes an informal speech about becoming an adult member of society. A large gathering of friends and family members enjoy eating, dancing, and having fun.

Jewish males and females are similarly feted at the age of 13. Their *bar-mitzvah* (for males) and *bat-mitzvah* (for females) symbolize the acceptance of the laws of Judaism and acknowledgment of the responsibilities of adulthood. The religious ceremony takes place in the temple, usually on a Saturday morning. Celebrants participate in reading the Torah (holy Hebrew scriptures), give speeches demonstrating their learning of Jewish principles, and thank their parents for bringing them to this important turning point in life. Festivities usually follow the religious service or later that evening with food, music, and dancing.

Among the Navaho of Arizona and New Mexico, initiates as young as seven and as old as 12 or 13 participate in a ceremony known as *Yeibichai* or "Night Way," which takes place outdoors around a burning fire. Although this is an awesome occasion for the initiates, it is also a time when adults make a lot of jokes at the initiates' expense.

Two assistant medicine men, one called Grandfather of the Monsters, wearing a white mask, and the other, Female Divinity, wearing a black mask, make marks with sacred cornmeal on the shoulders of each male initiate. During the ceremony, one at a time, the black-masked figure takes bound reeds and lightly strikes the cornmeal marks as well as other places on the boys' bodies while making a falsetto cry. The terrified boys, dressed only in loin cloths, startle, causing the crowd to laugh and joke. Observers shout for hard or light strokes for particular boys, but the masked figure always grants these requests in reverse while uttering a cry.

Females are treated differently. They remain seated and clothed with their blankets off. The figure with the black mask does not use reeds for the girls, but instead carries in each hand an ear of corn wrapped in spruce twigs which he presses against their cornmeal marks. After participating in other aspects of the ritual the children are told to look up and always remember the Holy People.

Sometimes tribal societies choose to circumcise their males as a mark of initiation into adulthood. The Arunta of Australia are a good example of this. After ritual singing and dancing, the elders wind strands of string around the boys' heads and place human hair girdles around their waists. The boys are then hidden away for three days where they receive instruction in the sacred lore of the tribe and learn Arunta myths and rituals. After the boys are circumcised they remain secluded until they recover. However, several weeks later a subincision ceremony (slitting the penis to the urethra with a stone knife) takes place, and once more the boys are secluded and engage in ritual pantomime and telling of tribal myths while they recover.

A variation of this ritual exists among Tahitians of Polynesia, where at a boy's coming of age an incision is made in the foreskin of the penis. From this time forward the initiate can no longer eat food cooked by women, nor can he eat in the company of women. Tattooing also takes place on this occasion.

CULTURAL RELATIVITY QUESTIONS

1. In your family at what age will you be considered an adult?

2. In your family or in your ethnic group how do you celebrate this rite of passage?

3. Can you say "Happy Birthday" in another language?

4. Do you know any other song sung at birthdays besides "Happy Birthday"? What is it?

5. How do you usually celebrate birthdays? Do you have cake, gifts, decorations? Do you have a party at home or go out? Do you celebrate with family only?

6. In your family, which birthday years are ones that have extra special celebrations?

7. Can you name some other kinds of ceremonies marking an important change in an individual's life; for example, a wedding?

8. Have you ever attended a rite of passage from an ethnic group different than the one you belong to? What was different about it?

9. In your family, what are some rights and privileges of being an adult?

10. In your family, what are some responsibilities of being an adult?

LEARNING MORE

The following related topics may be explored: rites of passage, *bar mitzvah*, *bat mitzvah*, *quinceañera*, Native American rites of initiation, rites of initiation of different societies in Africa, New Guinea, and elsewhere.

TELLING YOUR STORY

Choose one.

▲ Tell about a time when you were with someone who received a traffic ticket.

▲ Tell about a time when you were honored at a rite of passage (birthday, graduation, initiation into an organization, or another occasion).

▲ Write about a rite of passage that you witnessed (wedding, birthday, funeral, *quinceañera*, *bar mitzvah*, *bat mitzvah*, or another occasion).

TELLING YOUR STORY VARIATION

Choose one.

▲ Bring in a photograph of someone in your family being honored at a rite of passage. It can be a photo of a birthday, graduation, wedding, *quinceañera*, or other occasion. Tell your classmates the story about this occasion. Who is being honored? What is the occasion? Where did it take place? When? Can you see other elements of the ritual in the photo such as flowers, special clothing, presents, dancing, food?

▲ Today I Am a Man. Today I Am a Woman: Make a "Certificate of Adulthood." List the privileges. List the responsibilities.

TEACHING TIPS

No doubt students in your class will react as Carmen's classmates did and think it was "cool" that she could drive. This can lead to a discussion as to why rules and laws exist—for the protection of the public.

Stress that other countries have different rules based on different customs and circumstances, that what may be acceptable one place may not be so in other places. For example, in rural areas such as the Mexican countryside, where traffic is minimal and population sparse, it is not critical that drivers have licenses and learn complex rules. This is not unlike American farm children who drive big tractors and other heavy equipment, yet who need no licenses and have few restrictions in handling equipment far more dangerous than the car.

Elsewhere, countries may be more strict about issues that Americans are lenient about, as in Hong Kong, where if youngsters under the age of 16 are caught in a video arcade without an adult, they will receive a ticket.

Rites of passage examples should elicit lively discussion and good samples of cultural differences in your classroom. The objective is to point to the similarities, celebrate the differences, and convince students that because a custom is unusual or different doesn't make it less worthwhile.

Emphasize that societies everywhere recognize the significance of the move from childhood into adulthood and the responsibilities that this brings. Perhaps it explains the rationale for bringing gifts to the celebrant, whose life now will change and become more serious, complicated, and burdened with obligations.

You may want to audiotape or videotape the first Follow-Up Activity to focus on speaking skills.

The second Follow-Up Activity would work well either as a small-group discussion or whole-class board exercise to elicit opinions about obeying laws and why laws exist.

Cultural Relativity Question 7: Other rites of passage might include being born; graduations from grammar school, middle school, high school, college; confirmation; initiation into clubs; bridal showers; baby showers; getting a first job; retiring; and death.

SOURCES

Colvin, Richard Lee. "Art Meets Automobile at 'Blessing of Cars.' " *Los Angeles Times* (9 March 1992):B:1, 3.

Kluckhohn, Clyde, and Dorothea Leighton. *The Navaho.* New York: The Natural History Library, 1962.

Service, Elman R. *Profiles in Ethnology.* New York: Harper & Row, 1978.

Sherman, Josepha. *A Sampler of Jewish American Folklore.* Little Rock, Ark.: August House, 1992.

West, John O. *Mexican-American Folklore.* Little Rock, Ark.: August House, 1988.

UNIT NINE

THE INFLUENCE OF HEREDITY

NEW VOCABULARY

genetic   sponsored
heredity

SUBJECT MATTER

Genetic differences as the basis for cultural differences
Genetic differences in physical abilities, musical abilities,
    math abilities
Genetic limitations
Milk intolerance

ISSUES

▲ Cultural adaptations through imitation and
    trial and error
▲ Influence of cultural rules and customs that have been
    informally and unconsciously learned and accepted, yet
    rarely questioned
▲ What is acceptable and approved in one culture can be
    offensive or unacceptable elsewhere

WARM-UP QUESTIONS

▲ What special physical traits are found in your family
    (twins, color-blindness, blue eyes, red hair, baldness,
    missing teeth, gap-teeth, big toe smaller than the next
    one, tallness, shortness, dimples, all boys, all girls, other)?
▲ Are there any health problems that have been passed
    down through your family (weak eyes, diabetes, allergies,
    hay fever, asthma, other)?

Everybody Needs Milk?

My name is Linh, and I was born in Saigon, Vietnam, where I lived for almost half of my life until my family and I came to the United States in 1980. In Vietnam we don't have fresh milk to drink. Instead we have evaporated milk, and we only drink it once in a while or when we have a cold. My brother, sisters, and I were raised practically without fresh milk except for my mother's breast milk, which she fed us when we were babies. For this reason, many Asian people like my family are short and petite because they lack calcium that is needed for bones to grow and develop.

When we first came to Kentucky, my family was invited to a dinner given by the people at the First Unitarian Church. This was the same church that sponsored our move to America. The dinner was served with a variety of delicious foods. I noticed that each kid was served a large cup of fresh whole milk. Since I never had any fresh milk before, I hesitated to try it. While we were eating, we looked around to see if there was any water or soft beverages to drink besides milk. Of course, water and soft drinks were available at the dinner, but I was afraid to ask for them. I was afraid that since I was just a kid, I might offend the people at the church by not drinking the milk.

Anyhow, I was so thirsty from the salty food that I drank a whole cup of milk. I felt sick to my stomach right away. I went to the restroom a couple of times right afterwards. The people at the church all looked at me with confused faces and I didn't know what to do. I did not want them to think that their food or their cooking made me sick, so I told them the truth— that I was not used to drinking fresh milk.

I Felt Like I Was from Another Planet

After this big and most embarrassing event, my mother began serving us milk and she expected us to learn how to drink it daily because she said it was good for us kids. It took my brother, sisters, and me at least two weeks before we got used to it.

Thank you to the people at the church. Now we all know how to drink milk.

HEADLINES/OPEN MINDS

Write your answers inside the heads of the characters. You can use words, phrases, or pictures.

1. How do you imagine Linh felt when she saw the glass of milk by her plate? Describe her feelings.

2. What do you imagine the church members thought when they saw Linh rushing to the bathroom? Describe their different thoughts.

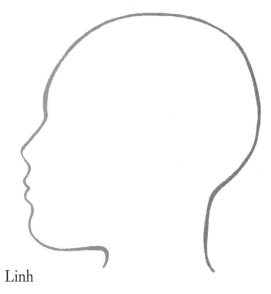

Linh

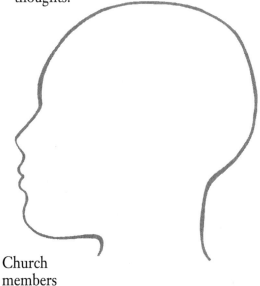

Church
members

3. How do you imagine Linh's mother felt when she saw Linh running to the bathroom more than once?

4. What do you imagine the church members thought when Linh told them about not being used to drinking milk?

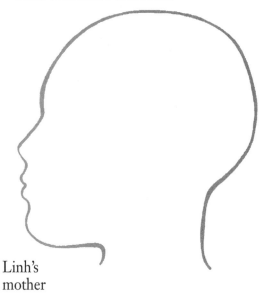

Linh's
mother

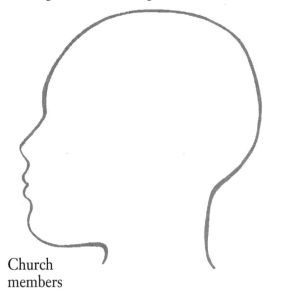

Church
members

OPINIONS AND IDEAS

1. Should Linh have drunk the milk at the church dinner? Why or why not?

2. Was it difficult or easy for Linh to explain to church members that she never drank milk before? Why?

3. In Linh's situation could you have explained to one of the church members that you were not used to drinking milk? Why or why not?

4. Have you ever been forced to eat something that didn't agree with you and made you sick? Explain your answer.

5. Should Linh's mother have started serving milk to her children? Why or why not?

FOLLOW-UP ACTIVITIES

1. Using marking pens or crayons, draw a detailed picture of yourself from your head to your feet. (You may want to look into a mirror to be more accurate about your face.) Include all of your physical characteristics: color and texture of hair, shape of face, color and shape of eyes, shape of eyebrows, shape of ears, attached or detached earlobes, shape of nose, shape of mouth, shape of chin, size and shape of hands and feet. Draw an arrow from each part that is like one of your family members and label it accordingly; for example, my mother's eyes, my father's feet, my grandmother's chin.

(*Note:* If you do not know anything about your birth parents' characteristics, draw a picture of someone else you know well and diagram the picture in relation to their family.)

2. Make a wish list. Write down characteristics of different family members that you wish you could have. For example, I wish I could be as tall as my father, as funny as my mother, as good in math as my sister.

CULTURAL BACKGROUND

The Dairyman's Association slogan notwithstanding, every body does not need milk. In fact, the United States is in a minority of worldwide milk drinkers. Globally ninety percent of Africans, American Indians, and Asians and ten percent of whites are unable to tolerate milk because they lack the specific enzyme (lactase) to digest it. Lactase breaks down lactose, a complex sugar found in milk.

Those who lack this enzyme experience symptoms ranging from bloating and abdominal cramps to severe diarrhea after drinking milk. If infants who are born with lactose intolerance syndrome (also called milk intolerance syndrome) are fed milk, in addition to pain and diarrhea, they may also suffer dehydration, malnutrition, and even death if correct diagnosis is not made.

Milk intolerance is not the same as an allergy. It is a genetic trait that accounts for the missing lactase. Lactase is present in all infants, allowing them to digest their mothers' milk, but after weaning the enzyme disappears in the majority of the world's population.

Lactose intolerance explains why Asian students experience stomach pains and diarrhea after drinking milk and dislike cheese and other dairy products. It also explains the presence in most supermarkets of a special kind of milk to assist those who lack the enzyme. Called Lactaid, this milk contains a reduced amount of lactose, and the lactase enzyme has been added. In addition to this product, tablets that contain lactase are also available, so that affected persons can chew them while ingesting dairy products or immediately following to avoid gastrointestinal discomfort. It is possible to learn to drink milk without a lactase supplement as Linh and her brothers and sisters did; however, only small amounts can be tolerated.

Milk intolerance is not a unique phenomenon. Another example of heredity causing a severe reaction to eating a specific food is found among certain people living in Sicily and Sardinia. They have an unusual physical reaction to fava beans, a staple food item of the area. Called favism, symptoms occur after either ingesting as little as only one seed of the fava bean or inhaling its pollen. This is also due to an inherited lack of a specific enzyme. Favism results in severe gastrointestinal complaints, malaise, headache, dizziness, fever, acute hemolytic anemia, vomiting, and diarrhea. Within approximately 24 hours jaundice occurs, which may lead to prostration and coma. Favism more commonly affects children, including nursing infants whose mothers have ingested the bean. Fortunately, sensitivity decreases over time.

The above physical disorders occurring after the ingestion of a common food are both genetically based. It may be useful to consider other diseases that are also genetically determined and seem to cluster around particular ethnic groups; for example, sickle cell anemia among

African Americans. In the United States approximately one in 1,875 African Americans have this disorder. Some may exhibit the disease, while others are said to be only carriers. It is also found among Mediterranean populations who originated in malaria-prone areas. Severity of the disease ranges from mild to severe, and symptoms include growth retardation, delay in secondary sexual development, leg ulcers, fatigue, gallstones, and stroke. Those affected may experience recurrent attacks of pain, and their life span is somewhat shortened. Infants who develop secondary infections are particularly at risk.

Another genetically determined disease is Tay-Sachs, found primarily but not exclusively among Ashkenazic Jews (those of Eastern European ancestry). There is also a noticeable incidence found among non-Jewish French Canadians living near the St. Lawrence River and among the Cajun population of Louisiana. Here history and genetics come together. In the early years of settling Louisiana many people were escaping previous lives, including Cajuns, former French Canadians who formed isolated settlements in rural Louisiana. There are two hypotheses to account for the incidence of Tay-Sachs among the Cajuns, who are mostly Catholic. One is that in the 1700s German Jewish and French Jewish settlers to the area might have brought the gene with them and passed it on to the Cajun population. The other possibility may be through a link with Spanish Jews who converted to Catholicism during the Inquisition and brought the gene with them when they resettled in Louisiana.

Tay-Sachs is a fatal disorder. The first symptoms are slowing of development in the infant, loss of vision, abnormal startle response, and convulsion. As the disease progresses, there is a deterioration of all functions, leading to blindness, mental retardation, paralysis, and death, usually by the age of three to four years. This disorder affects about one in every 2500 newborn Ashkenazic Jews. Approximately one in every 25 Jews in the U.S. is a carrier of the gene.

Finally, unexplained cases of sudden, unexpected nocturnal deaths have been documented by the Centers for Disease Control (CDC), and victims of this syndrome have all been Southeast Asians who have migrated to this country—Hmong, Laotian, Vietnamese, Kampuchean. It is not certain whether the cause is solely genetically based; there may be a psychosociological connection with their displaced persons status. Nonetheless there are related diseases in other Asian countries. For example, sudden nocturnal death syndromes have been recorded in Japan and in the Philippines, where the disease is called *bangangut*. The victims are usually male. They are in good health, are between the ages of 25 and 44, with few or none complaining of symptoms before going to bed. Sometime during the night they experience deep and labored breathing, and most die asleep in their beds. Almost all deaths have remained unexplained, even after thorough postmortem examinations.

CULTURAL RELATIVITY QUESTIONS

1. Do most members of your family have musical talents? Can they carry a tune or play instruments or dance well? Explain your answer.

2. Do most members of your family have athletic abilities? Explain your answer.

3. Do most members of your family have strong math abilities?

4. Do most members of your family have curly or straight hair? Do they have dark hair or light hair?

5. Are most members of your family able to whistle?

6. Can most family members roll up the sides of their tongues to form a trough?

7. Does double-jointedness run in your family?

8. Are the earlobes of most of your family members connected to the head or do they hang loose?

9. In your family are there some food allergies that several members have? What are they?

10. Do most members of your family wear glasses?

11. Are most members of your family quiet, shy, and reserved, or are they more outgoing and lively?

LEARNING MORE

The following related topics may be explored: genetics; heredity vs. environment; twins; chromosomes; genes (dominant and recessive); hemophilia; color-blindness; Down's syndrome; amniocentesis; DNA; Gregor Johann Mendel and his peas.

TELLING YOUR STORY

Choose one.

▲ Which aspects of your physical and personality characteristics do you think you inherited from specific family members? Explain whether you are pleased or displeased about this.

▲ When you are a parent, which physical or personality characteristics would you want your children to have from you or other family members? Tell why.

TELLING YOUR STORY VARIATION

Choose one.

▲ Give an oral report. Tell your classmates about how your brothers or sisters are like you, your parents, each other, or someone else in your family. If you are an only child, you can talk about yourself or choose a different family member to discuss.

▲ Divide a piece of paper into four sections and show yourself doing four different actions that are like another family member's actions (crying, being helpful, being mad, laughing, telling jokes, other). Caption each picture accordingly as if someone else were talking about you: "You're just like your grandmother—always talking on the telephone."

TEACHING TIPS

The first Warm-Up Question will be easier to deal with; the second may require more delicacy, depending on the makeup of the class. The sensitive aspect to be aware of is not to put students on the spot about their own or family health problems but to open up their awareness of the topic.

For the first Follow-Up Activity, it might be useful to have students bring small mirrors so that they can more closely examine their own facial features. This activity could also work well as homework, for which students could more accurately compare their physical characteristics with family members whose features they may have taken for granted.

To introduce the Follow-Up Activities, you may want to bring some of your own family photos to class to show the physical similarities between yourself and other family members. (Students seem to enjoy learning more about their teachers.) This will serve as a useful model.

To expand on this idea you may even want to have students bring in photos of themselves and family members to document in a more scientific way the effects of their family genetics.

The main goal of this unit is to show the effects of heredity upon one's physiology, personality, and behavior. The purpose is to help students develop a strong sense of family identity by exploring their own genetic background in a positive way. An additional aim is to raise their consciousness about how heredity can affect health through Linh's story of her milk intolerance.

You may want to emphasize how common an ailment milk intolerance is and how Americans are in the minority of milk drinkers in the world. Please note that neither milk intolerance or favism are considered the same as allergies.

The reason for focusing on genetic disorders or problems found among specific ethnic groups is to show how one's behavior may not always be based on choice. For example, Asian students refusing to eat pizza (because of the cheese) should not be chastised or accused of not wanting to be like the others. There is a physiological reason for their behavior. What is important is that other students learn that there are certain food intolerances that are based on physical, inherited characteristics. In addition, heredity need not only be expressed in negative ways. To give balance to the topic, the Cultural Relativity Questions focus on abilities and talents passed down through family genes. Pay tribute to these gifts.

SOURCES

Farb, Peter, and George Armelagos. *Consuming Passions: The Anthropology of Eating.* Boston: Houghton Mifflin, 1980.

Furst, George, ed. "Sudden, Unexpected, Nocturnal Deaths Among Southeast Asian Refugees." *American Journal of Forensic Medicine and Pathology* 3:3 (September 1982):277–79.

Kennedy, J. Michael. "A Tragic Legacy. Why Is Tay-Sachs, a Rare Genetic Disorder, Killing So Many Children in a Tiny Cajun Town? The Answer Seems to Lie in the Region's Melting Pot Heritage." *Los Angeles Times* (6 November 1990):E: 1, 3.

Lemoine, Jacques, and Christine Mougne. "Why Has Death Stalked the Refugees?" *Natural History* (November 1983):6–17.

Wynbrandt, James, and Mark D. Ludman. *The Encyclopedia of Genetic Disorders and Birth Defects.* New York: Facts on File, 1991.

AUDIENCE RESPONSE

NEW VOCABULARY

grito (scream)

SUBJECT MATTER

Being a performer
Cross-cultural ways of showing appreciation to performers

ISSUES

▲ Being embarrassed by parents
▲ Cultural adaptations through imitation and trial and error
▲ Emotional pain in becoming acculturated
▲ Understanding parents' difficulties as immigrants
▲ What is acceptable and approved in one culture can be offensive or unacceptable elsewhere

WARM-UP QUESTIONS

▲ Have you ever been embarrassed by something your parents did?
▲ Have you ever performed in a play or a musical group, danced, or given a speech? How did the audience respond?

El Grito

My name is Marisol, and I was born in Mexico where every day people wake up early in the morning. Before the bright sun has risen there are ladies shopping and cooking breakfast. On Sunday afternoons people attend church and walk around the plaza where there is a garden full of pink, red, yellow, and white roses with light green bushes. When the sun goes down, lights go on. Somewhere in the plaza sits a water fountain. Its water sparkles like shiny stars. The most beautiful thing in the plaza is the music. There is a feeling of dancing. You feel your heart warm. This feeling comes when you hear the people making happy *gritos* (screams). They sound like roosters crowing early in the morning. The *gritos* mean that you are happy, and you appreciate the song.

It seems like it has been forever since we left Mexico ten years ago. That's why I took my dad to see me play Mexican music at my American school. The performance took place in the auditorium where I was going to play my violin for the very first time.

The auditorium was full of parents coming to see their sons and daughters. We played many kinds of music, but when we played Mexican music, I saw a man stand up and do a loud *grito*. It was so loud that it made my hair go up. I couldn't see who that person was since there was darkness in the audience, but soon the auditorium was silent, and the lights went on. The school security guard walked over to the man who gave the *grito* and asked him to leave. The man looked familiar. I remember that it took me a while to realize that the man who did the *grito* was my father.

I Felt Like I Was from Another Planet

That night after the performance I tried explaining to my father that it wasn't right to do a *grito* in America, that if you like the music, you just clap. I don't know if he understood me, but after seeing everyone staring at him, I'll bet he won't do it again.

HEADLINES/OPEN MINDS

Write your answers inside the heads of the characters. You can use words, phrases, or pictures.

1. What feelings do you imagine Marisol had before playing her Mexican song at the school concert? List at least three.

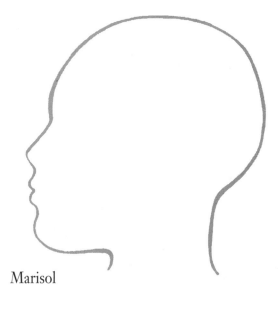

Marisol

2. What do you imagine the audience members thought when they heard Marisol's father do his *grito*?

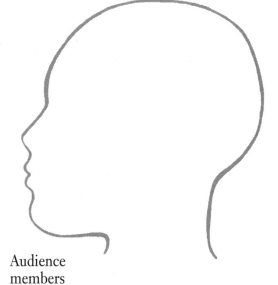

Audience members

3. How do you imagine Marisol's father felt when the security guard came over to him?

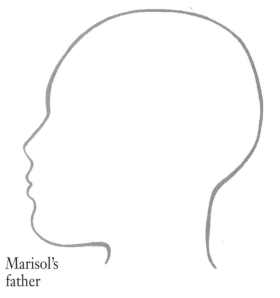

Marisol's father

4. How do you imagine Marisol felt when she had to explain to her father that in the United States you just clap if you like the music?

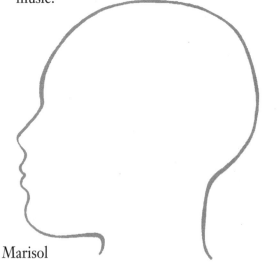

Marisol

OPINIONS AND IDEAS

1. What kind of relationship do you think Marisol has with her father? Why do you think this?

2. Should the security guard have asked Marisol's father to leave? Why or why not?

3. How does Marisol's description of the Mexican plaza make you feel? Does it remind you of any place that you know? If so, where?

4. What do think Marisol will say the next time she invites her father to hear her perform?

5. How will Marisol's father react the next time she invites him to hear her perform? Explain your answer.

FOLLOW-UP ACTIVITIES

1. Pick a partner and write a play about what happened to Marisol. You can change the ending if you like. Afterward, find three people to act out your play for the rest of the class.

2. Conduct a student survey. Ask two classmates either in this room or outside how many times they have attended the following live performances: symphony orchestra concert, play, puppet show, circus, rock music concert, ballet, dance performance, other. Compare your answers and see which form of live performance is the most popular in your age group.

CULTURAL BACKGROUND

In the United States, if you like the music you usually just clap after the music is over. That may be good advice for many audiences, but it doesn't necessarily apply to all American audiences. Some may give standing ovations and call out, "Bravo!" In addition, there are many ethnic variations in paying tribute to performers.

Among African Americans, African call-and-response behavior thousands of years old is still apparent in the ways in which the audience interacts with the performer. For an African American performer, a silent audience would be interpreted as a bored, disapproving one. Whether the audience is enjoying a concert, sermon, or political speech, it is customary and expected for them to let their reactions be known by clapping or shouting out commentary on what is heard as it is being presented. Often they are words of encouragement: "That's right!" "Yes, sir!" "Listen to him!"

Southern white audiences also display this demonstrative behavior, which has been affected by Southern Baptist Church customs and African American traditions. People will stand up during a rock concert and yell out, "Hell, yes!" "Hell, yes!"

For a Mexican audience, the roosterlike *gritos* are accepted and welcomed as an affirmation of the performance. This unusual sound, made in the middle of the music, has parallels with the utterances made by appreciative Middle Eastern audiences. Greeks will call out "*opaah!*" or "*yassou*" during a folk dance to encourage the performers.

Middle Eastern women make a trilling tone (ululation), vibrating the tongue against the roof of the mouth with a repetitive high-pitched "le, le, le, le, le" sound while cupping the hand over the mouth to control modulation. In Arabic, the term for this sound is *zagharid*. It is used during belly dances and other dance performances. You can hear these joyful sounds as well during weddings, when a woman gives birth, when a couple dances well, and at circumcisions. A similar sound of appreciation is used in some West African cultures.

An unusual form of audience participation and appreciation occurs in Indian audiences listening to classical music. Some members will "keep the tala"—maintain the rhythmic pattern of the musicians by counting on their fingers and clapping at particular intervals. The musicians consider this helpful. When pleased, the audience calls out, *"Bahut acchaa!"* ("terrific").

Whistling is a positive American audience response, but not in France, where it is used by disappointed audiences. In the U.S. the most frequent sound of displeasure is "boo."

An English woman once commented on the ridiculous (to her) behavior of American audiences who applaud a movie screen if they have enjoyed the film. From her British perspective, one only applauds a live performer. This same woman was also shocked at how quickly Americans jump to their feet to give standing ovations to "almost anyone." In Britain, she had been taught that this act of appreciation was reserved for only the most outstanding performers. She would be equally surprised to learn that members of the Writers Guild of America west (professional movie, radio, and TV writers) must promise that they will not hiss, boo, or talk back to the movie screen if they wish to be members of the film club society.

In British music hall and military tradition, when the audience is sitting at tables, they will bang the tables with their mugs as a sign of enthusiasm. Similarly, during speeches they will thump the tables and yell out "Hear! Hear!" "Well done!" or "God bless the Queen!"

The audience for the Indonesian *wayang kulit* (shadow puppet play) has a different set of behaviors, because this very popular form of outdoor entertainment lasts from 9 P.M. until sunrise the next day. Consequently audiences sleep during the performance, eat, talk, and smoke clove cigarettes. At particularly engaging scenes they will hoot and clap enthusiastically.

Audience behavior varies not only because of geography and ethnicity but also with the type of entertainment. For example, at American athletic events, especially baseball games and some rock concerts, the audiences spontaneously do "the wave," in which one section at a time stands up and sits down in unison. When the adjacent section repeats that action going in sequence around the stadium, it creates a wavelike motion to onlookers attending the event or watching on TV. However, in the 1990s the popularity of this behavior seems to be waning.

At British rock concerts and at American punk concerts happy audience members will "gob" (spit at) the performers. At Japanese rock concerts the audience will only applaud politely. As described by one rock and roll musician, "They act just like a school assembly audience." In striking contrast, at the 1992 Michael Jackson Dangerous Tour in Bucharest, Romania, the audience screamed, fainted, and stood and swayed with arms outstretched in a manner reminiscent of Beatles fans in the 1960s and Frank Sinatra followers in the 1940s.

CULTURAL RELATIVITY QUESTIONS

1. In your family, are you permitted to whistle or stamp your feet when you are happy with a performance? Explain.

2. In your family, are you permitted to boo when you are displeased with a performance?

3. When you go to the movies do you talk in the theater?

4. Have you ever been to a live music performance? What kind? Where did it take place?

5. What is your favorite kind of listening music?

6. Do any of your family members (including yourself) take music lessons? If so, what kind?

7. Do you like to listen to music on the radio? What station do you listen to?

8. Do you like to listen to music on CDs or cassettes? What is the name of the last title that you purchased?

9. Do you ever sing at home? Do you sing by yourself or with others? Do you sing while listening to or playing music? Do you sing to karaoke?

10. Have you ever spoken, acted, danced, sung, or played a musical instrument in front of a live audience? Give details.

TELLING YOUR STORY

Choose one.

▲ Tell about a time when your parents embarrassed you.

▲ Tell about a time when you were a performer (gave a speech, danced, sang a song, played a musical instrument). How did the audience react to you?

▲ Tell about a time when you were part of an audience and the performer did something unexpected or the audience did something unexpected.

TELLING YOUR STORY VARIATIONS

Choose one.

▲ Make an advertisement poster for a performance you would like to star in—for example, as a dancer, an actor, rap artist, rock singer, concert pianist, member of a hip hop band, other. Tell where you are going to perform, when it will take place, who else will appear with you, and the cost of tickets. You might want to include a drawing of yourself giving your star performance.

▲ Write the words to a song that might be sung about the story topics above. The song might consist of two- or four-line verses, and you might want to add a chorus.

TEACHING TIPS

This unit will allow you to pay tribute to the performing arts. Through the Cross-Cultural Questions you will no doubt discover who has musical abilities or who takes lessons.

If you discover that students, their parents, or siblings study or perform music, stage a classroom musical event. Before the concert talk about the ways in which you, as an audience, will show your appreciation to the presenters.

You might even be fortunate in discovering that one of your students is studying an ethnic instrument or singing or dancing style. If ethnic presentations are going to take place, encourage those students to wear national dress. This would be an excellent way to pay tribute to cultural diversity and to show the performers that these skills and talents can be appreciated outside the ethnic community. By so doing, the musicians' self-esteem will be increased and the audience's knowledge expanded.

The *grito* given by Marisol's father caused her embarrassment, particularly because he was so exposed in the suddenly lit-up auditorium and ejected by the security guard. Note, however, that Marisol never expresses any anger toward her father. She understands that his mistake is caused by cultural differences. That Marisol doesn't reveal any resentment indicates a kind of maturity on her part.

Marisol's family situation is typical of many immigrant and refugee families. Often the children learn the rules of the new culture more quickly than the adults in the family. Certainly this applies to language acquisition. It is much easier for immigrant children to learn English than their parents and grandparents. It is also easier for the children to adapt to American culture.

The unfortunate effect of this is that immigrant fathers, who once were in a position of authority in their homelands, often lose their status within the family here. This occurs not only because of the inability to learn the new language, but also because of not being able to pursue occupations held in their native countries. Frequently, the wives find employment more easily (doing domestic or needle work) while the husbands remain unemployed. When the women and children have more social and economic power than fathers, these role reversals lead to intergenerational conflicts. This can cause breakdowns in the physical and mental health of family members.

Children adapt more easily to the new culture because of school. Through imitation and trial and error they learn the do's and don'ts of this culture. Thus, the classroom becomes an environment for acculturation, the place to acquire more than learning skills. By being with culturally diversified classmates, newcomer students ideally can become better equipped for living in a multicultural society. Meanwhile their classmates can learn from them, as well, especially if teachers promote understanding and appreciation of cultural differences. It becomes apparent that the teacher has a potentially powerful role as a culture broker.

The first Follow-Up Activity is a good exercise in collaborative writing and the writing of dialogue. Consider videotaping the presentations.

SOURCES

Axtell, Roger E. *Gestures! The Do's and Taboos of Body Language Around the World.* New York: John Wiley & Sons, 1991.

Gold, Steven J. "Mental Health and Illness in Vietnamese Refugees." *The Western Journal of Medicine* 157:3 (September 1992):290–94.

Pliskin, Karen L. "Dysphoria and Somatization in Iranian Culture." *The Western Journal of Medicine* 157:3 (September 1992):295–300.

UNIT ELEVEN

GAMES

SUBJECT MATTER

Competition vs. cooperation
Games
What games reveal
What we learn from games
Winning and losing

ISSUES

▲ Emotional pain in becoming acculturated

WARM-UP QUESTIONS

▲ What are your favorite sports?
▲ What kinds of games do you like to play with your friends at home?

Play Ball!

I am My and I was born in Vietnam but raised in Hong Kong where I lived for nine years. Therefore I am more used to Chinese culture than American culture even though I immigrated here almost five years ago.

Because there is a shortage of land in Hong Kong, students have fewer opportunities to participate in certain kinds of sports which need large fields or gymnasiums. In addition, students in Hong Kong do not bother with various kinds of sports because physical education does not count as an important subject. As a result, I ended up learning about sports by watching and not by playing.

Actually, when I first attended high school in the United States I never realized that playing sports had the same value as studying. In my P.E. class when I was still a freshman I suddenly discovered that there was such a game called "baseball." People who grew up here knew how to play the game, but for me, playing baseball caused so much trouble and embarrassment that I will remember it forever.

I believe the teacher assumed that I knew how to play baseball. Therefore, she did not explain the rules of the game or how to play it. Instead she just placed me on one of the teams. I was a new student and also had communication problems with my teammates. Consequently, they told me to stay on the left side of the field and catch the ball. Actually, I had nothing to do in my position except watch them having so much enjoyment with the game. However, I knew that I would have a turn to be a pitcher because each student had to play each position.

Finally, I had a chance to hold up the bat and hit the ball. But to tell the truth, I had no idea how far to hit it and

© Addison-Wesley Publishing Company, Inc.

why my teammates kept running after they hit the ball and stopped at a certain place on the field. Accidentally, I hit my third ball; at that moment I tried to run as fast as I could, but I did not know where I should stop, so I ran back to where I stood before. After I completed this procedure, all of my teammates started laughing at me, but I did not understand what I had done wrong. Eventually, one girl approached me and said, "Hey you, stupid! Don't you know to stop at the base?" At that time, I did not want people to think I was a nut, so I just signalled to her that I understood what she meant.

Although I had baseball for almost six weeks and never did understand the rules of the game because of my mistake, my teammates would not let me go to bat anymore. The lesson I learned from baseball was that people should not be thought of as stupid for what they do not know. However, this was a good experience for me, even though I did not enjoy the game. Now as I am writing this, I understand that to learn a new culture, I must ask questions about what I don't know and learn from my mistakes.

HEADLINES/OPEN MINDS

Write your answers inside the heads of the characters. You can use words, phrases or pictures.

1. How do you imagine My felt when she was first put on the left side of the field? List the different kinds of feelings.

2. How do you imagine My's teammates felt when she hit the ball, didn't know where to run, and returned to home plate? List at least three feelings.

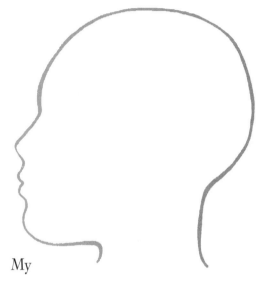

My

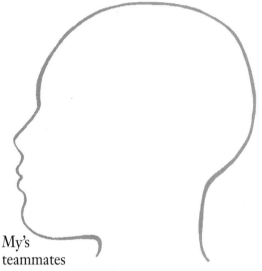

My's
teammates

3. How do you imagine My felt after six weeks of baseball?

4. What are some of the feelings you have had when playing a sport or a game that you were not good at?

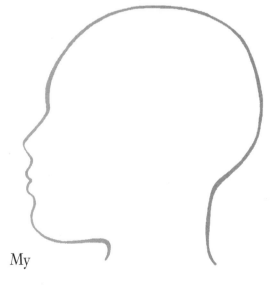

My

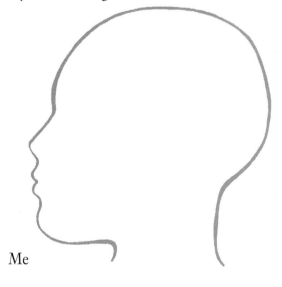

Me

OPINIONS AND IDEAS

1. Should physical education classes be required and graded? Why or why not?

2. Do you enjoy playing organized sports at school? Why or why not?

3. What do you think about My's teammates not letting her go to bat after she made her mistake?

4. What should My's teacher have done about the situation?

5. Make up a different ending to this story.

FOLLOW-UP ACTIVITIES

1. Tell this same story, but this time tell it from the teacher's point of view. Do this in comic strip form. In simple pictures inside boxes, show what happened to My when she went up to bat. Write balloon dialogue over the different characters' heads—My, the teacher and the other students.

2. Get into small groups, with a mixture of boys and girls in each group, and write down the rules for playing baseball. How many players are needed? How are they divided? What is the point of the game? Can you name the positions? How is the game scored? Who wins? How many rules can you list?

CULTURAL BACKGROUND

Baseball is considered America's national pastime. The passion for this game reveals Americans' respect for individual achievement and team competition. Every fall American fans wait to see which are the winning teams, who will win the World Series, who is the most valuable player in each league, who has the highest batting average, who pitched the highest number of strikeouts, and so on.

Baseball exemplifies one of the attributes that many Americans value—individual performance—even on a winning team. This should not be surprising, because games reveal what is important to a society. Games also teach a society's values.

Not all societies value individuality as Americans do. Some societies prefer cooperation and teamwork in daily life. Consequently, their games reflect this preference. For example, in Lancaster County, Pennsylvania, one Amish school board has forbidden the use of baseball gloves and regulation balls at school. Instead, the children play with a sponge ball or another soft ball and without gloves. By changing the rules, the Amish make baseball less competitive and discourage young people's desire for worldly methods and materials. The idea is to prevent dependence for goods in their adult lives.

Another example of a noncompetitive attitude in play is found among the descendents of former African American slaves who live on the coastal islands off Georgia and South Carolina. Instead of aiming for the exhibition of individual skills and achievements, their games stress general participation. They have no winners and very few losers. Instead of complying with strict game rules, they prefer dramatic interpretation and re-enactment of real-life dramas such as catching chickens, quarreling with mothers, finding love partners, and working.

In these sea island communities, games involve both music and dance, with hand clapping as the only musical accompaniment. The hand clapping is so complex that by varying the shape and tension of their cupped hands, players can clap in three tonal ranges—bass, baritone, and tenor. Along with hand clapping there is often an intricate contrapuntal foot-stamping rhythm pattern. This reflects the call-and-response musical traditions of Africa that have influenced this population. The result is a moving, joyous, creative outlet for the players.

While cultural differences may account for different games found in different locations, they may also affect the ways in which the same games are played differently, reflecting distinct social values. Witness the difference between Japanese and Americans. In contrast to Americans, who emphasize winning, the Japanese aim for the most correct form. For example in golf, getting the right swing, the right stance, and the right shot is more important than getting the best score. Here form is paramount, reflecting an important Japanese value.

Sometimes games and sports are intertwined with religion and the seasons and related especially to the agricultural cycle. In Korea, New Year's Day is the most important calendar celebration. To mark this occasion in rural areas, large scale Tug-of-War contests are held. An entire village will divide into two teams according to the cardinal directions. One team is symbolically female and the other male. The female team must eventually win in order to guarantee a productive year. This event has spiritual roots as well as important social significance, and villagers begin preparing weeks in advance of the celebration. In some places whole counties may participate with as many as 10,000 men on a team. The Tug-of-War traditionally lasts from three to four days, from 11 A.M. to 11 P.M., with half-hour rest periods of singing and dancing.

The Apache's most important game is the Hoop and Pole. It, too, has a religious character, and in the past no festivity was complete without it. Hoop and Pole is played by men only, two at a time, each with a pole representing the two sexes. The object of the game is to take turns throwing hoop and poles toward three parallel ridges eight to ten feet in length. The hoop and poles must be propelled in such a way as to land in the depressions between the ridges and stop before they pass the extreme ends of the ridges.

Several short prayers and charms are sung or spoken to bring success to one's self and to diminish the opponent's power. Here is the translation of one:

The wind will make it miss yours.

The wind will turn it on my pole.

Today at noon I shall win all.

At night again to me will it fall.

In 1901 an observer wrote that the Hoop and Pole was played by Apache men every day from early morning to late in the afternoon. Sometimes it was merely to pass the time. Sometimes it was used as medicine, but always it was played for gain, and players sometimes bet everything they had on the game.

Although some games have printed official rules, especially in organized sports such as baseball, football, hockey, basketball, and soccer, a large body of games is learned informally from parents, siblings, and friends. Some games have been passed down in this way through the centuries and are found all over the world.

Playing games begins in infancy. For example, parents and grandparents everywhere play variations of Peek-a-Boo, This Little Piggy, and Horsey. The games are played to cultivate rapport with children, to stimulate their senses, and to subtly test and develop their reflexes and alertness.

Besides being entertaining, all games are learning vehicles. As children grow older, some games teach them counting and the alphabet. Other games teach hand-eye coordination (hand-clapping games, jacks, and marbles), body coordination (jump rope, hopscotch), decision-making and problem-solving strategies (hide and seek).

Today, with the popularity of television as an entertainment, children spend more time sitting and watching rather than participating in games. Video games blend these two interests. Although critics bemoan the emphasis on violence in video games, the games also nurture competition and develop hand-eye coordination and decision-making skills.

Despite high-tech video games, children and adults engage in games from around the world that are centuries old: card games, dice games, board games (chess, checkers, parchesi, mah jong, and backgammon).

CULTURAL RELATIVITY QUESTIONS

1. Name some outdoor games you play out of school.

2. Name some indoor games you play when you are not in school.

3. Do you or does anyone in your family play on a sports team of any kind? Describe it.

4. Has anyone in your immediate or extended family ever won an award for being an outstanding player in game or sport?

5. Does anyone in your family play any kind of card game or board game? Describe it.

6. What kinds of jumprope games and songs do you know?

7. What kinds of hand-clapping games do you know?

8. What kinds of hopscotch games do you know?

9. Demonstrate one kind of hand-clapping game, chanting or singing the words you know.

10. What do you learn from playing some of your favorite games?

LEARNING MORE

The following related topics may be explored: games; sports; pastimes; history of particular games: mah jong, parchesi, chess, Rubic's cube, Monopoly, dominoes, card games, others.

TELLING YOUR STORY

Choose one.

▲ Tell about when you won a game, contest, lottery, or prize.

▲ Tell about when you expected to be a winner (of a contest) or expected to be the top person or best person and you were not.

▲ Tell about participating in a sporting event that was exciting and explain what it was like.

TELLING YOUR STORY VARIATION

Create an award you would like to receive. The award can be a certificate or the drawing of a trophy in the shape of an Oscar, loving cup, or any other design. Be sure to include important information on the award: your name, date received, what the award is for (best dancer, winner of the spelling bee, top student in the class, best player on the team, or any other field in which you would like to be a winner).

TEACHING TIPS

A good point to emphasize is why My's teammates were more concerned with winning than with My's feelings. Why didn't anyone feel sorry for her or even ask why she behaved the way she did? Here is a situation in which neither classmates nor teacher stepped in to help My.

Is winning everything? When one person wins, how do the others feel? This is a question that can be explored after the story and the follow-up questions. Try to get students to reveal their feelings about losing. While this might prove painful, it is also useful for them to understand that others have the same feelings when they don't win. You might examine how attitudes toward winning develop over time. Continuous emphasis reinforces winning as an ideal and the ultimate goal.

Here are other questions you might want to raise: How do you feel about winners? Do you get jealous? Are you able to share in the winners' happiness? Can you congratulate them? Deep down, do we all resent the winners in life because they did it and we didn't? How do you overcome feelings of resentment? How difficult is it to be a good sport?

And how does it feel to be the winner? Is it really lonely at the top? While the moment of glory might be thrilling, is it worth it to win if others will be jealous of you? For example, in the Filipino workplace and in certain other cultures, people are often reluctant to be promoted because it destroys the peer relationships they once had.

Another area to explore is what the payoff is regarding games. What do we learn from them? With professional sports, winning equals money, which equals power. It doesn't pay to be a loser. From organized sports we also learn that teamwork is important, we learn about strategy and decision making, and we learn that discipline and exercise keep us physically fit.

The first Follow-Up Activity provides a good opportunity for students to think about alternative points of view and therefore examine motivations for behavior. For example, why didn't the teacher help My with her problem that lasted six weeks?

The second Follow-Up Activity will reveal how much or how little students know about baseball rules. This may help them develop more empathy for My.

The answers to Cultural Relativity Question 10 could lead to a discussion of the following issues: teamwork; competition; building physical skills; gender and occupational role modeling; development of aggression.

The Telling Your Story Variation can create a vicarious pleasure and might even inspire students to aim for a real award.

SOURCES

Botermans, Jack, Tony Burrett, Pieter van Delft, and Carla van Slunteren. *The World of Games*. New York: Facts on File, 1989.

Collins, Robert J. *Japan-Think Ameri-Think: An Irreverent Guide to Understanding the Cultural Differences Between Us*. New York: Penguin Books, 1992.

Culin, Stewart. *Games of the North American Indians: Volume 2: Games of Skill.* Lincoln, Nebraska: University of Nebraska Press, 1992. (Reprint of the 1907 edition published as *The Twenty-Fourth Annual Report of the Bureau of American Ethnology*, 1902–1903, Smithsonian Institution.)

Fisher, Sara E., and Rachel K. Stahl. *The Amish School.* Intercourse, Pa.: Good Books, 1986.

Jones, Bessie, and Bess Lomax Hawes. *Step It Down: Games, Plays, Songs, and Stories from the Afro-American Heritage.* New York: Harper & Row, 1972.

Knapp, Mary, and Herbert Knapp. *One Potato, Two Potato . . . The Secret Education of American Children.* New York: W. W. Norton 1976.

Sutton-Smith, Brian. *The Folkgames of Children.* Austin, Texas: University of Texas Press, 1972.

Wood, Clement, and Gloria Goddard. *The Complete Book of Games.* New York: Doubleday, 1940.

Yarfitz, Denise. "Traditional Korean Games." *Korean Culture* 5:1 (March 1984):16–29.

UNIT TWELVE

TEACHERS AND STUDENTS

SUBJECT MATTER

Classroom discipline
Culturally different education systems
How we learn
Oral tradition
The role of students
The role of teachers
Written tradition

ISSUES

▲ Cultural adaptions through imitation and trial and error
▲ Emotional pain in becoming acculturated
▲ What is acceptable and approved in one culture can be offensive or unacceptable elsewhere

WARM-UP QUESTIONS

▲ What was the worst thing you ever saw a teacher do to a student?
▲ Have you ever thought one of your teachers was too strict? Too easy?

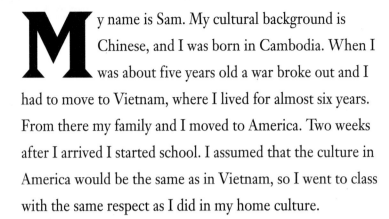

Rules and Rulers

My name is Sam. My cultural background is Chinese, and I was born in Cambodia. When I was about five years old a war broke out and I had to move to Vietnam, where I lived for almost six years. From there my family and I moved to America. Two weeks after I arrived I started school. I assumed that the culture in America would be the same as in Vietnam, so I went to class with the same respect as I did in my home culture.

I was put into the fourth grade but I wasn't able to speak any English, and I didn't understand a word anyone said. Everyone was a stranger to me because I didn't know what they were saying. At recess I went out knowing nobody. Suddenly one of my classmates held my hand and pulled me to play games with her and some other classmates. The only problem was that it was a girl asking me to join her and her friends playing jump rope. When I attended school in Vietnam, boys were supposed to play with boys and girls played with girls. I didn't understand what she wanted, so I went along and played.

The class was noisy. Everyone was painting. I painted too, but suddenly I accidentally knocked the water on the floor and paint spilled all over. Everyone called Ms. Elkins, our teacher, and when I looked at her she seemed to be mad at me. She called me up to her table by waving her hand. I then went to the chalkboard and picked up a ruler. I gave the ruler to Ms. Elkins and put my hand out for her to hit me.

Ms. Elkins didn't know what I was doing. I was frightened because in Vietnam when you did something wrong, you had to go and pick up a ruler for the teacher to

I Felt Like I Was from Another Planet

hit you. Afterward, you had to stay in a corner until the teacher told you to sit down. I assumed that this school was the same.

The teacher didn't know what I was doing and the students laughed at me. Ms. Elkins didn't hit me. Instead, she put the ruler away, then took me by the hand to get some paper towels to clean the floor. She talked to me, but I couldn't understand her, so instead she showed me how to clean the floor.

This situation was very embarrassing, but it was a great learning experience for me. I learned not to act the same way in America as in my culture. I feel that Ms. Elkins put in a lot of time to help me out and I learned a great deal from her.

HEADLINES/OPEN MINDS

Write your answers inside the heads of the characters. You can use words, phrases, or pictures.

1. How do you imagine Sam felt when he couldn't understand or speak the same language as his classmates? List his feelings.

2. How do you imagine Sam felt when he spilled the water and paint? List his feelings.

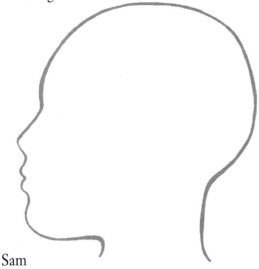

Sam

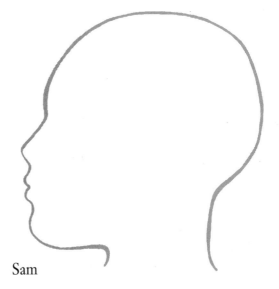

Sam

3. What do you imagine the other children thought when they saw Sam hand the ruler to the teacher?

4. What do you imagine Ms. Elkins thought when Sam handed her the ruler? List some of her thoughts.

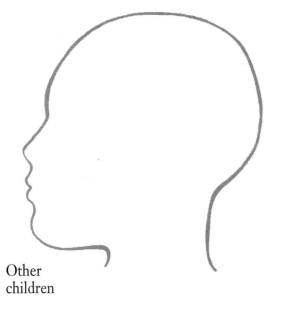

Other
children

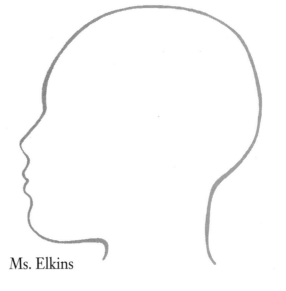

Ms. Elkins

OPINIONS AND IDEAS

1. Is it better to have boys play only with boys, and girls play only with girls during recess activities at school? Why or why not?

2. Why did the students laugh at Sam when he handed Ms. Elkins the ruler?

3. Do you think teachers should be able to discipline students by using a ruler or some other form of physical punishment? Why or why not?

4. How do you expect Ms. Elkins will react the next time a new student from a different country spills something or makes a mistake?

5. If you could advise American teachers about how they could become better teachers, what would you tell them?

FOLLOW-UP ACTIVITIES

1. If I Were the Teacher: Get into groups of two or three students and decide what you would do about the following classroom situations if you were the teacher.

▲ A student keeps interrupting classroom activities by clowning around.

▲ A student accidentally spills paint on the floor.

▲ A student picks on another student who is physically different.

▲ A student always arrives late, but it's the parent's fault and the parent doesn't seem to care.

▲ A student is very smart but doesn't do his or her work and seems bored.

▲ A student physically fights with others.

▲ A student cheats.

2. With a partner make a list of school rules you think are fair and another list of rules that you think are unfair. Compare your list with the lists of your classmates.

CULTURAL BACKGROUND

When we think about education, we often think of a classroom with a teacher standing in front of students giving instructions. We tend to forget that by the time children reach nursery school or kindergarten they understand their native language and have learned to construct and communicate meaningful, correct grammatical sentences. What's more, they have absorbed rules of behavior and values from family members and friends, and enter preschool armed with opinions.

In pre-reservation days before they had written language, Western Apache tribe members were forced to remember what was recited. Learning stories and prayers was how information was passed from one generation to the next. Stories of brave men and their deeds were recited at evening meals and told exactly for they had been carefully memorized. Children who would later become leaders learned the tales by hearing them repeated numbers of times. This is called learning by oral tradition, as opposed to learning by written tradition.

The Amish, a religious community with about 90,000 members in the United States, have a unique educational system that when challenged was upheld by the U.S. Supreme Court in 1972. According to their beliefs, children need not go to school beyond the eighth grade, and their private country schools are taught by non-college-trained teachers, generally single Amish women—never men. The goal of these schools is to prepare the children for usefulness in life as well as eternity, so religious teachings are incorporated into the curriculum.

The Amish use one-room schoolhouses, located so that no child has to walk more than two miles to school. One teacher has 40–50 pupils, and she teaches four subjects, with emphasis on reading, writing, and arithmetic. The native language of the Amish is a dialect of high German similar to that spoken in the Palatine or Rhineland regions of modern Germany. Consequently, when children first start school, they learn to speak English through phonics. If children do not behave in class it is acceptable for teachers to spank their behinds with their hands or with a stick.

When the children finish with their eighth-grade education they continue learning at home. Girls learn homemaking skills; boys learn farming methods so that by the time they are 17 or 18, they know animal husbandry, crop rotation, and farm finances.

Traditional Vietnamese education was influenced by the Chinese as well as the Colonial French. Consequently, scholars and teachers are highly respected. The teacher is thought to know everything and is considered to be the source of knowledge and wisdom. Conversely, the teacher's responsibility is to preserve the cultural heritage by honoring books and thereby faithfully transmitting the cultural heritage from one generation to the next. The students' responsibilities are obedience, quietness, and respect. Therefore, students must listen respectfully, repeat the information, and memorize and recite lessons. When a discipline problem occurs, the teacher can use a bamboo or rattan stick to strike the child.

Pure Chinese educational traditions are similar. The teacher is the absolute authority, and the teacher expects complete attention. Learning is based on memorization through reading textbooks or by copying the teacher's explanation from the board. This sometimes causes a problem for American teachers working in China, who often discover that American methodologies don't transfer well to China. American teachers look with favor upon independent work, small group discussions, and interactive exercises such as simulation games. These techniques are not always successful in China.

American education nurtures the formation and articulation of opinion regardless of what the teacher might think or what the textbook says. Americans assert that students can have fun while working and learning. Teachers encourage creativity and independent thought because originality and independence reflect American cultural values.

Compare the American system with that of the Japanese. Japanese children have 240 school days in a school year (as opposed to 180 in the U.S.) and go to school six days a week. Education in Japan is so important that getting into the right nursery school can determine the child's ultimate adult job with a particular corporation or choice of marriage partner. As a result, there is keen competition at each level of schooling and children go to cram schools where they spend two to twenty hours per week preparing for tests to gain entrance into the next educatonal level. High school students can spend as many as 60 hours a week preparing for college entrance exams.

As with other Asian systems of education, in Japan learning is based on fact memorization. Since individuality and creativity are not goals for the students, it follows that creative and innovative teaching methods are likewise discouraged.

CULTURAL RELATIVITY QUESTIONS

1. What have you learned from your mother?

2. What have you learned from your father?

3. What have you learned from your brothers or sisters?

4. What have your friends or classmates taught you?

5. What have you learned from television?

6. What have you learned from books?

7. What have you taught somebody else? Describe it.

8. What other languages do you speak? Who taught you?

9. What do you learn by going to the mall?

10. Do you plan to go to college? Why or why not?

TELLING YOUR STORY

Choose one.

▲ Tell about the best teacher you ever had.

▲ Tell about the worst teacher you ever had.

▲ What is the most important skill you ever learned?

TELLING YOUR STORY VARIATION

Use two lunch-size sacks to make two hand puppets, one for each hand. One represents you and the other a teacher you once had or now have. Decorate the puppets using marking pens, crayons, buttons for eyes, other objects for facial features, yarn for hair, fabric remnants, or other materials.

When finished, give a presentation with your puppets, re-enacting a memorable experience you once had with a teacher who was either very good or very bad, or re-enact something funny that happened between a teacher and you.

TEACHING TIPS

Talk about Sam's teacher, Ms. Elkins, how kind she was to him that day in school and later in the semester once she realized how little he understood English. You might want to ask students if they have ever been in a similar situation where they didn't understand the language, the rules, or the customs. You might also inquire if students have ever witnessed something similar to Sam's situation. Encourage discussion as a means to develop empathy for those with limited English language skills. Ask if anyone in your class has ever tried to help someone with language limitations. What happened? How did they feel helping another person?

The first Follow-Up Activity is a good example of having students "put the shoe on the other foot," allowing them to experience teachers' common dilemmas. You may be surprised, as well, by how their solutions compare with yours. This activity provides an excellent opportunity to air students' opinions about teachers who are hard, easy, kind, or unfair. You might want to ask them what makes a good teacher. Likewise you can move on to ask what makes a good student—one who is quiet and obedient and does his or her work, or one who does good work, but may disagree with the teacher?

For this first Follow-Up Activity you could have groups work on the same problems to see if their solutions are the same or different. Or you could give each group just one problem to solve and then have them compare their solutions.

Entries on the unfair list for the second Follow-Up Activity will offer you an opportunity to explain the rationale behind them. You could also ask the students to speculate on the reasons fair and unfair rules might have been made.

The main idea behind the Cultural Relativity Questions is to make students aware of the importance oral tradition and imitation have played in what they know. They see that they already have acquired a vast body of information, attitudes, and opinions through an informal yet powerful learning process. Emphasize that they are not blank slates when they arrive at their kindergarten doors; instead they are already storehouses of knowledge and values.

Students have learned important lessons while sitting in the kitchen observing or helping a parent cook or clean up; they have recorded signficant data from their brothers or sisters while doing chores; they have absorbed social values from the games they play; they have gained valuable knowledge while handing their parents tools to fix something. Remind them that they, too, have been teachers by showing someone how to do something. Explain that when they come to school they are slowly switching modes of learning, from oral to written methods, and how much more significant the written word will become as they advance in their schooling.

In giving answers to Cultural Relativity Question 9, students can learn about fashion trends, costs, who else frequents the mall besides shoppers (seniors, police, young people looking to meet the opposite sex), and shopping behavior. Do people shop alone? Do they shop with others? Do shoppers mostly buy with cash or use credit cards? What kinds of other activities are there? Is there entertainment? Are there product or cultural demonstrations or art exhibits?

The Telling Your Story Variation would be an excellent activity to preserve on videotape. You can use it to renew the discussion at some later time.

SOURCES

Ball, Eve, with Nora Henn and Lynda A. Sanchez. *Indeh*. Norman, Ill. and London: University of Oklahoma Press, 1988.

Collins, Robert J. *Japan-Think Ameri-Think: An Irreverent Guide to Understanding the Cultural Differences Between Us*. New York: Penguin Books, 1991.

Fisher, Sara E., and Rachel K. Stahl. *The Amish School*. Intercourse, Pa.: Good Books, 1986.

Hostetler, John A. *The Amish*. Scottdale, Pa.: Herald Press, 1982.

Lingxin, Zhang. "Linguistic Problems or Cultural Assumptions." *CATESOL News* 19:1 (June 1987):15.

Martinez, Jimmie, and Arlene Watters, eds. *US: A Cultural Mosaic: A Multicultural Program for Primary Grades*. 823 United Nations Plaza, New York, NY 10017: ADL of B'nai B'rith, n.d.

Warner, James A., and Donald M. Denlinger. *The Gentle People: A Portrait of the Amish*. P.O. Box 217, Lititz, Pa. 17543: Lititz Office Products, Lititz Bookstore, Lititz Office Furniture, 1964.

UNIT THIRTEEN

FAMILY LIFE

NEW VOCABULARY

chores

SUBJECT MATTER

American children seem to be spoiled or have an easier life than children elsewhere

Attitudes toward children

Child-raising customs

Child-raising customs as a reflection of world view

ISSUES

▲ Cultural adaptations through imitation and trial and error

▲ What is acceptable and approved in one culture can be offensive or unacceptable elsewhere

WARM-UP QUESTIONS

▲ What household chores are you expected to perform?

▲ Do you receive an allowance for doing household chores?

Chores

I come from a Mexican family, and my name is Karina. Both of my parents were born and raised in Mexico, but I was born in California. I have been living here all my life. Since I was raised in this country my customs and beliefs are somewhat different from those of my parents.

My cousin Martha was born and raised in Mexico. She is about three to four years older than me. She was brought up in a totally different environment than mine. The customs that one goes by in Mexico are totally different than those of California. I consider myself more modern and lucky.

In the summer of 1989 my sister Linda and I went to Mexico to spend the whole summer there. It had been six years since we had last visited Mexico. At that time I was only 13 years old and Linda was seven. We stayed with my grandfather from my father's side. It was a totally different environment for both of us. We were not used to the way the children were raised there.

When I met my cousin Martha I was real surprised to see what her chores consisted of from the time she woke up to the time she went to sleep. Tía Ester, Martha's mom and my aunt, owned a store, so Tía spent most of her time attending the customers and keeping the shelves stocked. Martha then had most of the responsibilities at home. She had to wake up at 6 o'clock in the morning and go to the mill to bring back nice freshly-made corn tortillas for breakfast. She would then attend the store while my aunt served the family breakfast. Martha would eat and continue her chores by washing the dishes and the clothes by hand. As soon as noon came around she would again go to the mill and get

I Felt Like I Was from Another Planet

more tortillas. After eating lunch she cleaned up the house and could only go visit her friends if everything had been done at home.

All that was a shock to me because in Mexico the parents depended on their daughters to do most of the chores. Yet I was not brought up that way. At my house in the U.S. we were all given a chore or sometimes even more than one, yet it was still my mother's responsibility to do the greatest portion of work. I tried to explain to my cousin that in Los Angeles we would buy the corn tortillas and keep them refrigerated and that all we did was put some soap in the washing machine and then wait for the machine to stop. My cousin looked at me with this look on her face that seemed as if she were going to eat me up. She looked at me from top to bottom and from bottom to top. I didn't know what I had said to get her like that.

That is when everything happened. That day I was wearing a black skirt, white blouse, nylons and some white shoes. My cousin was wearing a brown skirt, orange blouse and some black sandals. My other cousin, Juan, was just stepping into Martha's room with a friend of his. Martha told Juan what I had just told her about the way we did our chores here in Los Angeles. In a shocking way she made fun of me.

Both Juan and his friend began to laugh at me. I remember Martha saying, "Well, look honey, just because you live in L.A. does not make you special here. The special thing about a woman is her knowing how to do things and not depending on machine-made things." At that point I felt like it was the end of the world because they were making fun of me. I felt useless and what bothered me most was the fact that I still had to be there about a month and a half more. At that moment I just wanted to call my parents up and tell them that I wanted to go home, yet I knew that I had to prove to my cousins that I could do things, too.

That is when I went to my grandfather's house and spoke to one of my unmarried aunts. I explained what happened. She told me that the girls from there were jealous of the girls from L.A. That is why my cousin had acted that way with me. That made me think differently. I decided that I wasn't going to let myself be laughed at. I then asked my aunt if she would teach me some of the things that one does in Mexico. My aunt agreed. She taught me to wash clothes by hand, go to the mill to get freshly-made tortillas, and I learned quite a few other things that I would never have been able to do or learn in Los Angeles.

One day Martha came over to see why I hadn't been to her house. She then saw my aunt and me washing clothes and saw me helping with other chores. Martha looked at me and came up and told me that she was sorry. She hadn't meant to laugh at me. She just didn't realize that we were in different environments. She smiled and said, "I guess you don't have to be raised in Mexico to be special." I was so happy that I felt little butterflies in my stomach. I was glad that I was accepted for who I was and not rejected because of where I came from. I felt my eyes watering yet I held my tears in for I was happy and not sad. I now look back at that incident and see it as a valuable experience.

HEADLINES/OPEN MINDS

Write your answers inside the heads of the characters. You can use words, phrases, or pictures.

1. How do you imagine Martha felt watching Karina and Linda doing nothing while she herself worked so hard?

2. How do you imagine Karina felt when Martha, Juan, and his friend laughed at her?

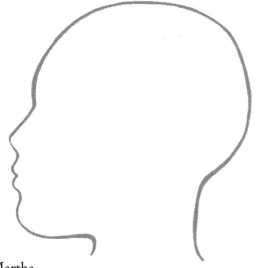

Martha

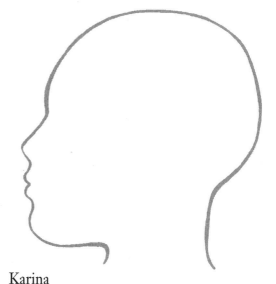

Karina

3. What do you imagine Karina's aunt thought when Karina asked her to teach her what girls do in Mexico? List at least three thoughts.

4. How do you imagine Karina felt when she returned to the United States and was expected to do only the few household chores she had done before?

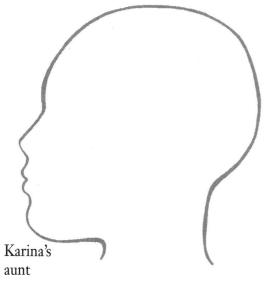

Karina's aunt

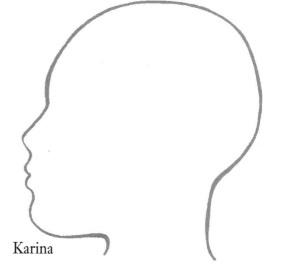

Karina

OPINIONS AND IDEAS

1. Do you agree with Martha that the special thing about a woman is knowing how to do things and not depending on machine-made products? Why or why not?

2. Do you agree with Karina's aunt that Martha was jealous of Karina? Why or why not?

3. Do you feel sorry for Martha because she has so much work to do? Why or why not?

4. Do you think that once Karina returned home she went back to her old ways of doing very few household chores? Explain your answer.

5. Do American-born children have it too easy? Why or why not?

FOLLOW-UP ACTIVITIES

1. Make a list of chores you do in your home. Compare your chore list with that of a classmate. Do most of your classmates have similar types of chores? Or do some chores involve more responsibility than you have?

2. Meet My Family: Draw a picture of each member of your family who lives in your household. Use a separate piece of paper for each person. Write down the person's name and list all the family responsibilities that each member has.

CULTURAL BACKGROUND

Babies born into the Hutterite community, a communal branch of the Mennonite Church located in South Dakota and Canada, are loved and welcomed by the immediate family and community. Although infants are the center of attention at birth, by two months of age, the socialization process begins. According to Hutterite religious beliefs, the child's will must be broken and must bend to the will of God. For example, although infants are constantly coddled and pampered, when it is time for adult meals or for church they are left alone in their cribs. Toilet training begins as soon as the child can sit. Walking and weaning also start early. Children are taught not to fight or use bad language; they are encouraged to love all community members and are warned about the hazards of greed and private property.

Misbehavior results in punishment by hand, strap, or switch. By the time they are fifteen, Hutterite children no longer attend school, play with children, or perform children's chores. Instead they do adult work and take their place in the adult dining hall.

Similarly, in pre-reservation days Western Apache adults in Arizona and New Mexico taught children from the age of six all that they would need to know as adults. Consequently, by the age of 12 the children took an active part in obtaining and preparing food. Gradually they increased their adult responsibilities. However, after reservations were established, children were expected to be in school much of the year and therefore could not participate in the economic life of the tribe.

Unlike the the Hutterites' leaving children alone in cribs, many other societies carry their children with them at all times. This is one of the purposes of Native American cradle boards, pieces of wood to which babies are strapped and toted everywhere by their mothers. For example, in New Mexico, Acoma babies are kept on cradle boards until they walk. A U.S. government agency representative once suggested putting a playhouse in a proposed Acoma nursery school facility. Parents objected, however, when they saw that the playhouse equipment included a crib. Acoma families never use cribs for their children.

Cradle boards have several functions. They keep the children close by at all times—an obvious advantage for nomadic people—and they keep curious infants restricted in movement and thus out of harm's way. Among the Acoma there is an additional benefit. In this tribe, cradle boards are made of wood taken from trees that have been struck by lightning. Since the Acoma believe that lightning never strikes twice in the same place, the cradle board offers double security for the child.

Akin to the properties of the cradle board is the custom of swaddling babies (keeping the baby tightly wrapped in blankets or sheets) for up to two years. Like the cradle board, swaddling keeps the baby snug and warm and restricts the child from exploring dangerous environments. There are other explanations for this custom, which is very popular throughout Eastern Europe and Iran, where it is believed that swaddling allows babies to save their energy for when they grow up.

Among the Klamath River Indians of Oregon, babies are weaned within a month. Mothers do this by placing hot spicy peppers on their own nipples. From this experience, children learn that they can't trust others—not even their own mothers. Similarly, when these infants are strapped to their cradle boards they are secured very loosely, which reinforces their insecurity and distrustfulness.

An extreme example in contrast to the Klamath River Indians is found in the way Israelis treat children. When the dream of creating a Jewish homeland was being conceived, one of its founders, Theodor Herzl, was convinced that in a new country children must come first, and their survival must be paramount if the country were to survive. This was in striking contrast to the strongly patriarchal societies of Europe that most Israeli settlers came from.

Herzl believed that there must be a deliberate change in family practices in order to guarantee survival of the Jews. The future and success of the new country would depend upon the younger generation—both boys and girls. As a result, when the kibbutz became a reality, children's quarters were the first built and were erected in the safest location; children were of primary concern and care; when it came time to serve food, children received theirs first; in the children's quarters the most qualified mothers and teachers were chosen to make them feel secure.

Later, when forced to live in underground shelters year round because of enemy attack, the children continued their art lessons; the Israelis maintained as much stability in the children's routine as was possible. All these behaviors reveal the Israelis' understanding that the only way the culture could continue would be if the children survived physically and emotionally.

Through child-raising customs and attitudes (giving of love and affection, feeding, swaddling, weaning, toilet training, disciplining, teaching responsibility and discipline, instilling a sense of dependence or independence) parents prepare their children for adulthood. By practicing these customs, societies reveal their world view. Certainly a connection must exist between societies that restrict their babies' movements and the social restrictions the babies are expected to encounter as adults.

Americans do not practice swaddling. Is this because they encourage their children to explore and develop their own self-identity? Although the delegation of very few household responsibilities might be interpreted by some as permissiveness and irresponsibility, it might also be seen as nurturing freedom and individuality.

CULTURAL RELATIVITY QUESTIONS

1. In your family, are you expected to do household chores for free, or do you receive an allowance for doing them?

2. In your family, are older brothers and sisters expected to work and contribute part of their paycheck to the family?

3. In your family, do parents or children get their food served first?

4. In your family, if you get an allowance, can you spend it all or must you put a certain amount away to save?

5. When you shop for clothes do you or your parents decide what to buy?

6. In your family, must older children obey the advice about what major to take in high school or college?

7. In your family, do parents listen to the children's problems and offer advice?

8. In your family, do parents listen to advice from the children?

9. In your family, is the oldest or youngest child the one with the most privileges?

10. In your family, does the mother do most of the household work or do the children? Explain your answer.

LEARNING MORE

The following related topics may be explored: child-raising customs around the world: breast feeding, bottle feeding, weaning, swaddling, cradle boards, toilet training, children's responsibilities; discipline; child-development theories of T. Berry Brazelton, Jerome Bruner, Robert Coles, Eric Erikson, Jerome Kagan, Jean Piaget.

TELLING YOUR STORY

Choose one.
- ▲ Tell about a time when you were expected to complete a chore or task that you were not able to do.

▲ What do you think your family will be like in twenty years? What will you be doing? Where will you be living? Will you be married and with children?

TELLING YOUR STORY VARIATION

Choose one.

▲ My Family Is Special. List the ways in which your own family is special.

We are the _____family.
(family name)

We have_____

_____

_____
(list members)

We do these special things: _____

_____

_____

_____

We like these special things:_____

_____

_____

We know these special people:_____

_____

We want_____

We can _____

We eat _____ for special meals.

We help each other_____

_____

_____

▲ Draw a picture of what you think your family will look like in 20 years. Where are you in this picture? What are you doing? What are other family members doing?

TEACHING TIPS

At the end of Opinions and Ideas you may want to discuss the following issue. From Martha's point of view, Karina was spoiled and had it too easy. Does it harm children to let them have too easy a life? Should children have a carefree childhood because later on as adults they will have to be responsible for themselves and others? Will childhood be their only time to have fun? Or are children better off having responsibilities early in life so they can be prepared for the future? The answer to this question may be culturally determined. Yet it could stimulate a lively and fruitful discussion. Students of all ages should be able to participate easily. This question will also make them feel important since they will be discussing what generally is considered an adult question.

The Cultural Relativity Questions are more personal than those in preceding units, but if you choose this unit as a later one, the students should be accustomed to the format and style. Students might feel embarrassed about answering some of them, especially when their own families seem quite different from those of their classmates. To cushion this feeling, you may want to remind students that how parents treat their children is actually culturally determined. Therefore it may be useful for you to share some of the information contained in the Cultural Background section.

Explore the issue in the second Warm-Up Question by asking, "Should children be given a monetary reward for doing household chores or should chores be an accepted part of family participation and not something that should be financially rewarded?"

Paper for the second Follow-Up Activity can be cut in different sizes in proportion to the size of the person, from two to eight inches. After all the families have been created the students can display the pictures as a group or put them on a bulletin board.

The first Telling Your Story Variation promotes pride in one's own family. Students may complete it in class or take it home and have family members assist them.

The second Telling Your Story Variation projects students into the future, allowing them to consider, perhaps for the first time, that they have options to change or continue with their current family patterns. This may be particularly useful and comforting to those experiencing unhappiness at home. This exercise may empower students to make choices in their family life when they become adults.

SOURCES

Erikson, Eric. *Childhood and Society.* New York: W. W. Norton, and Co., 1950.

Ferg, Alan, ed. *Western Apache Material Culture: The Goodwin and Guenther Collections.* Tucson, Ariz.: University of Arizona Press, 1987.

Hostetler, John A. *The Amish.* Scottdale, Pa.: Herald Press, 1982.

Kephart, William M. *Extraordinary Groups.* New York: St. Martin's Press, 1976.

Martinez, Jimmie, and Arlene Watters, eds. *US: A Cultural Mosaic: A Multicultural Program for Primary Grades.* 823 United Nations Plaza, New York, NY 10017: ADL of B'nai B'rith, n.d.

Oz, Amos. *The Seventh Day.* New York: Vintage, 1984.

FEMALES AND MALES

SUBJECT MATTER

Differences in education and career expectations for females and males

Differences in general treatment of females and males

ISSUES

▲ Being caught between parents' old world customs and American customs and values

▲ Going against parents' rules

▲ Stereotypes

▲ Understanding parents' difficulties as immigrants

▲ What is acceptable and approved in one culture can be offensive or unacceptable elsewhere

WARM-UP QUESTIONS

▲ In what ways are boys or men treated better than girls or women?

▲ In what ways are girls or women treated better than boys or men?

Sugar and Spice?

My parents were both born and and raised in Vietnam with Chinese customs. In the Chinese tradition, boys are always better than girls. I believe the Chinese think that way because at home they are always against girls doing what they want.

Our family came to America ten years ago when I was about nine. I consider myself raised in America because before coming to the United States I lived in three different countries for a few years. America is the place where I have lived the longest and I think of it as my home. I even gave myself an American name—Jennifer.

In America I go to school and learn like everyone else. I have learned to treat everyone equally regardless of sex, age, or color, but at home I'm treated differently. My parents believe that boys are better than girls. Maybe it is because my dad was raised that way and my mom didn't have any education; she can't read or write.

My parents believe that girls should have just enough education to get a job and bring money home for them, and boys should have an education—the more, the better. In addition, according to Chinese custom, when a girl gets married, it means that she is no longer the daughter of the father. She is now considered the father's half daughter, and whatever she does or has belongs to her husband's side of the family.

I understand how they think and I respect them for what they believe, but I also wish that they would understand and respect my beliefs. For example, my brother, Henry, opened a sewing factory last summer. Because he is new in the business and knows nothing about it, he needs help. I can

I Felt Like I Was from Another Planet

sew very well because for a few years during high school I worked for my other brother Paul in his factory. My sister Emma knows how the business runs and where to get materials. That is why my dad expects both Emma and me to quit college and help Henry with the business.

My dad never thinks about us. All he cares about is my brother. He said that both us girls have enough education already and that we should help Henry because he doesn't have the education that we have. My dad knows that because Henry is a high school dropout, he won't find any work. My father never stops to think that I just graduated high school and Emma has only one more year until she receives her B.A. degree.

If we listened to my dad and helped Henry, I probably would end up sewing for the rest of my life, and I hate sewing. And my sister would have to waste all those years that she worked so hard for her B.A. degree. And when my brother and father made money or became rich they would probably throw us out and say we were useless anyway.

In our home, the boys don't have to do anything because it's all girls' jobs. The housework is all done by me or my mother because Emma moved out last year to live with her friends. I feel like a slave at home. My mom cooks. I set the table, get what my dad and brother want, clean up the table and wash the dishes. I remember when I had fights with my brother, my dad always hit me first. After all these years, I don't really care what they think or do anymore. All I know is that I have to take care of myself. Whenever my dad has something to say to me, I just listen and go back to my room.

I hope to graduate as soon as possible and be what I want to be as long as I'm happy and take care of myself. If I don't, no one will. What I have today is all owed to myself.

HEADLINES/OPEN MINDS

Write your answers inside the heads of the characters. You can use words, phrases, or pictures.

1. How do you imagine Jennifer felt when her father asked her to quit school to help her brother? List at least three feelings.

2. What do you imagine Jennifer's father thinks when Jennifer refuses to quit school? List some of his thoughts.

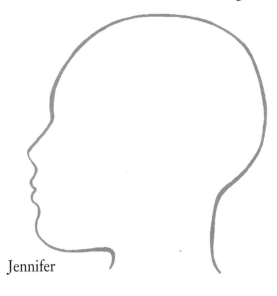

Jennifer

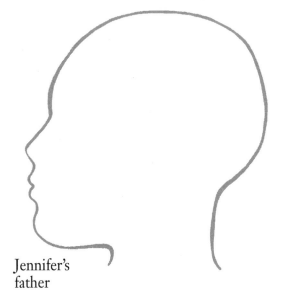

Jennifer's father

3. What do you imagine Jennifer's brother Henry thinks about his sisters when they refuse to work in his factory?

4. How do you imagine Jennifer feels toward her father and her brother? List some of her feelings.

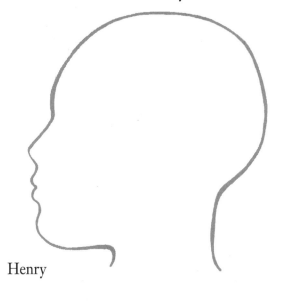

Henry

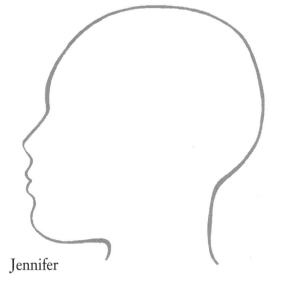

Jennifer

© Addison-Wesley Publishing Company, Inc.

OPINIONS AND IDEAS

1. Does Jennifer's mother sympathize with her daughters? How do you know this?

2. Is Jennifer right in not wanting to help her brother in his factory? Why or why not?

3. Is there any other way that Jennifer could help her brother? How?

4. What do you predict will happen between Jennifer and her family after she graduates college?

5. Do you know other families where girls seem to be treated unfairly?

FOLLOW-UP ACTIVITIES

1. Either as a general classroom board activity or in small groups review some favorite fairy tales (Cinderella, Snow White, Sleeping Beauty, Hansel and Gretel, Red Riding Hood, Jack and the Beanstalk, others) and compare the ways in which females and males are portrayed.

Who is powerful? Who is weak?

Who needs help? Who solves problems?

Who takes action? Who needs saving?

Who is good? Who is evil?

After discussing the answers, move on to these questions:

According to the portrayal of females and males in these fairy tales, which would you rather be?

If children grow up listening to these stories, what will they think about girls compared to boys?

Do you think these stories have been told for centuries because the stories reflect the differences between the ways girls and boys actually behave? Is there another explanation?

Do these stereotypes still apply or are they changing? Give examples.

2. Check off the following activities you would not engage in because you are a girl or boy.

BECAUSE I AM A GIRL
I would not
_____ climb a tree
_____ play baseball
_____ go hunting
_____ beat a boy at sports
_____ ask a boy out for a date
_____ do repairs around the house

BECAUSE I AM A BOY
I would not
_____ cry
_____ wash dishes
_____ kiss my father
_____ hit a girl
_____ play with dolls
_____ sew a button on my shirt

Now add more activities you would not do because of your sex.

CULTURAL BACKGROUND

"Ladies, shall we leave the gentlemen to their brandy and cigars?" This cliché from old movies showing the female dinner guests adjourning to another room reflects common attitudes regarding differences in the ways men and women are treated. In most societies in the world, baby boys are greeted with much more favor and joy than are baby girls. For example, in traditional Iranian culture when a boy baby is born, family and friends will compliment his beauty and describe him as golden—a creature of the highest value. When a baby girl is born, parents are told, "At least she's healthy, thank God!"

Perhaps the best known and most extreme preference for boys comes from ancient China, where boys were always the favored sex and female infanticide was not unusual. In general, these attitudes prevail the world over, but there are exceptions. For example, among the Zuñi Indians of New Mexico girls are more desirable than boys. The Zuñis fear that if a man is in the house during a child's delivery, his presence will turn the unborn girl into a boy. Thus men are unwelcome at the time of birth.

The man has traditionally been thought of as husband, provider, and head of the family, while the woman was the wife, mother, keeper of the house, and caretaker of the children. American women have fought hard to change those popular perceptions, particularly since they don't match the reality of 1/6 of all American families. According to the 1990 census,

10,666,043 families are headed by women with no husbands present.

In contrast, among the Hutterites (a communal branch of the Mennonite Church numbering about 4000, found in South Dakota and Canada), women cannot hold office or serve on the church council or vote on community issues. When discussions and decisions are to be made, women are excused from business meetings. Furthermore, women are not permitted to drive vehicles. In the dining hall, they sit at their own tables, and at church services they sit in their own section.

Many Orthodox Jewish sects also separate the sexes. Women sit apart from the men in the synagogue; during wedding celebrations the women and men are segregated from each other and do not dance together. In public, social interaction between the sexes is disapproved.

Evidence that males are considered the more privileged sex is found in some rural areas of India, where only boys are allowed to go to school. A nursery school teacher reports on a difference found in the way a Japanese mother treated her fraternal twins. When the mother packed lunches for her children, the son received a scrambled egg sandwich sweetened with jelly, but his sister had her scrambled egg sandwich without the sweetener. The boy got something extra, something special. This small act reveals the dramatic discrepancy in the ways the different sexes are treated. Boys need the best to make them strong, and it's acceptable for girls to get what's left. This division of rights continues into adulthood: Japanese males are allowed off elevators first, are served first in restaurants, and walk ahead of their wives. Early on, males learn to see themselves as privileged and females see themselves as less significant.

CULTURAL RELATIVITY QUESTIONS

1. In your family, how are household chores divided between girls and boys? Are there some tasks that only fathers do? Are there some that only mothers do?

2. In your family, are there certain sports that only girls or only the boys can engage in?

3. In your family, are girls expected to achieve as well as boys in school?

4. In your family, are there certain careers and professions that only girls can have and others that only boys can have?

5. In your family, can girls date at the same age as boys? Can they go out on dates alone?

6. In your family, will parents have the same influence over the selection of the son's marriage partner as they will over the daughter's marriage partner?

7. In your family, will the married sons or married daughters be expected to live with their parents?

8. In your family, will the sons or daughters be expected to care for sick or elderly parents?

9. In your family, are the opinions of the girls valued as much as the opinions of the boys?

10. When you get married and have your own family, will you treat your sons and daughters in the same ways as your parents have treated you? What changes will you make?

LEARNING MORE

The following related subjects may be explored: Gloria Allred, Corazon Aquino, Clara Barton, Hillary Rodham Clinton, Madame Curie, Amelia Earhart, Betty Friedan, Indira Gandhi, Corita Kent, Georgia O'Keefe, Golda Meir, Christa McAuliffe, Margaret Mead, Rosa Parks, Sally Ride, Margaret Thatcher, Gloria Steinem, Mother Theresa, ERA, MADD, NOW, WACs, WAVEs, 19th Amendment.

TELLING YOUR STORY

Choose one.

▲ Tell about a time when you did something just because you thought it was the right thing for a girl or boy to do.

▲ Tell about a time when you didn't do something because you didn't think it was the right thing for a girl or boy to do.

▲ Tell about a time when you were asked to do something because you were a girl or a boy.

▲ Tell about a time when you were not allowed to do something because you were a girl or a boy.

TELLING YOUR STORY VARIATION

Using two pieces of paper, label one sheet "Female Jobs," and the other "Male Jobs." Divide each sheet into four sections and in three of the sections draw an appropriate job for a person of that sex. In the fourth section of each sheet draw a person doing something unexpected for their gender; for example, a female airline pilot and a male secretary.

TEACHING TIPS

You might want to begin with the title, "Sugar and Spice" and ask the students if they know the nursery rhyme that begins, "What are little girls made of?"

What are little girls made of?

Sugar and spice and everything nice—

That's what little girls are made of.

What are little boys made of?

Snakes and snails and puppy dogs' tails—

That's what little boys are made of.

Ask the students what they think is the significance of this nursery rhyme. You may want to discuss how girls are thought of as sweet, pretty, virtuous, and ornamental while boys are perceived as wild, active, and earthy. What happens if girls want to be earthy, wild, and mischievous? Will society allow them to be? What happens when a female wants to be something different from what her family expects? How difficult will this be for her and for her family?

The same applies to boys. How will families react if boys are disinterested in sports and prefer more quiet activities? What happens if boys want to play with dolls, the kinds that girls usually play with?

In discussing Jennifer's situation, generational and cultural differences are apparent. Jennifer will have many problems if she continues with her Americanized ways. Ultimately she may be estranged from her family.

This issue may be useful to show students an extreme example of parent/child conflict. In American society some conflict with parents is expected and subtly condoned. However, parents may complain when their children actually become independent. This stands in striking contrast to cultural groups in which children spend their lives paying respect to parents and accepting traditions without question.

Help your students develop empathy for both sides: the parents, who are continuing with the only way they know and what they consider is the right way, and Jennifer, who is in the difficult position of being caught between two very different sets of cultural rules. Talk about the strength and pain that Jennifer has because of her position and decisions.

You might want to raise the question as to whether there are times when an older child must break parents' rules. This can be followed up by asking what circumstances might cause a child to do this. However, to maintain some balance, be sure to help students also acknowledge that conflicts with parents don't necessarily cause loss of love or respect.

Both Follow-Up Activities deal with the issue of stereotypes and how in today's world others' limited expectations for either boys or girls also handicap the child's development, self-esteem, and productivity. In discussing the first Follow-Up Activity, ask, "Could it be that these stories are told to instruct the different sexes how they should behave?"

In discussing the first Cultural Relativity Question, you may want to ask if fathers can be as good nurturers of children as mothers. Should fathers participate in feeding, changing, bathing, and dressing of infants and older children?

SOURCES

Babcock, Barbara A., ed. *Pueblo Mothers and Children: Essays by Elsie Clew Parsons 1915–1924*. Santa Fe, N. M.: Ancient City Press, 1991.

Collins, Robert J. *Japan-Think Ameri-Think: An Irreverent Guide to Understanding the Cultural Differences Between Us*. New York: Penguin Books, 1992.

Hostetler, John A. *The Amish*. Scottdale, Pa.: Herald Press, 1982.

Kephart, William M. *Extraordinary Groups*. New York: St. Martin's Press, 1976.

Shiman, David A. *The Prejudice Book: Activities for the Classroom.* 823 United Nations Plaza, New York, NY. 10017: ADL of B'nai B'rith, 1979.

United States Department of Commerce Bureau of Census. *1990 Census of Population and Housing, Summary Population and Housing Characteristics.* United States: 1992, 3.

Wald, Carol, and Judith Papachristou. *Myth America: Picturing Women 1865–1945.* New York: Pantheon Books, 1975.

UNIT FIFTEEN

PREJUDICE

NEW VOCABULARY
complexion

SUBJECT MATTER
Living in a multicultural society
Prejudice

ISSUES
▲ Accepting someone who is different from yourself
▲ Being kind to a stranger
▲ Standing up for someone else
▲ Stereotypes
▲ Xenophobia

WARM-UP QUESTIONS
▲ Have you ever been the victim of prejudice because of your physical appearance, age, religion, or ethnicity?
▲ Have you ever met someone different from yourself and you expected them to behave in a certain way, but they surprised you?

Monsy and Michelle

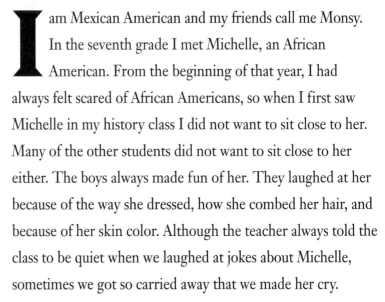

I am Mexican American and my friends call me Monsy. In the seventh grade I met Michelle, an African American. From the beginning of that year, I had always felt scared of African Americans, so when I first saw Michelle in my history class I did not want to sit close to her. Many of the other students did not want to sit close to her either. The boys always made fun of her. They laughed at her because of the way she dressed, how she combed her hair, and because of her skin color. Although the teacher always told the class to be quiet when we laughed at jokes about Michelle, sometimes we got so carried away that we made her cry.

At first I made fun of her too, but only because I didn't want other students to make fun of me. Since I have a brownish complexion, I thought they would probably make bad jokes about me, too. After two weeks I got tired and sad that some students still continued to make fun of her. The following week I began to sit next to her.

Michelle was surprised and smiled at me. Everyone in the class was shocked. They began making fun of me. They told me that I was dirty like her, that we were black because we didn't take showers. I felt very bad and I began to cry. I got so angry that one day I stood up in class and shouted at the other students. They all stood quiet. I told them that it wasn't fair to make fun of people because of their appearance and culture. In fact, Michelle was the smartest student in class. Michelle was so happy I stood up for her that we became very good friends.

Through this experience I learned that all people are the same no matter what they look like. I learned that because of the different cultures we have in this country we

I Felt Like I Was from Another Planet

can learn many new things that help us have a more interesting life. By speaking out and proving to others what you are able to do, you can make a difference. Michelle and I found out that each human being is unique in appearance, but may feel the same inside. As a result of this experience I learned not to be scared towards colored people or those from different cultures.

HEADLINES/OPEN MINDS

Write your answers inside the heads of the characters: You can use words, phrases, or pictures.

1. Imagine how Michelle felt when her classmates made fun of her.

2. What do you imagine were Michelle's thoughts when Monsy sat down next to her?

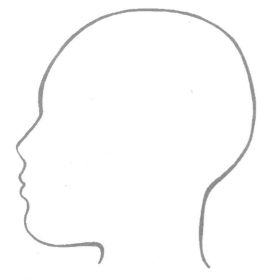

Michelle

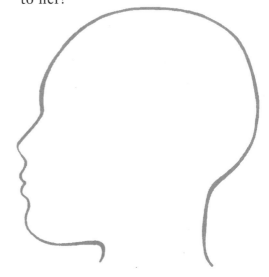

Michelle

3. What thoughts do you imagine the other students had when Monsy sat down next to Michelle?

4. How do you imagine the other students felt when Monsy shouted at them? List at least three feelings.

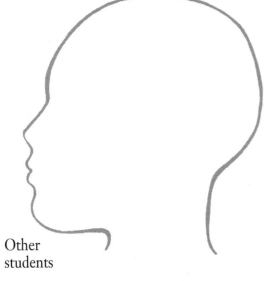

Other students

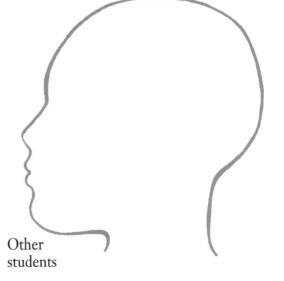

Other students

OPINIONS AND IDEAS

1. If Michelle had been an African American male instead of a female, do you think the other students would have acted the same way? Why or why not?

2. How might the teacher have improved the situation after Michelle cried?

3. What do you think about Monsy standing up for Michelle? What does this tell you about her character?

4. Could you have done what Monsy did? Why or why not?

5. After this experience will Monsy's classmates treat African Americans the same way as they treated Michelle? Why or why not?

FOLLOW-UP ACTIVITIES

1. Find two objects from nature, such as two leaves from the same tree, two rocks, two peas from the same pod, two kernels of corn from the same cob, or two flowers of the same kind. Make a list of how these two objects are the same and how they are different. Look at them for a few minutes every day for at least three days and keep adding to your list of similarities and differences. What can you learn from this?

2. Watch at least one hour of television and note the following information. Write down the name of show and the major characters. Then make a chart like the one on page 164. Add other categories if they appear in the show.

Answer the questions by marking in the appropriate column.

Based on your findings, which group would you want to belong to?

How would you feel if you were a member of a group that was negatively portrayed?

	YOUNG	OLD	WHITE	AFRICAN AMERICAN	LATINO	ASIAN AMERICAN	NATIVE AMERICAN	MALE	FEMALE
Who are the villains?									
Who are the heroes?									
Who seeks help from other people?									
Who solves the problems?									
Who is smart and can do things well?									
Who is dumb and not able to do things well?									
Who is afraid?									
Who is wealthy?									
Who is poor?									

CULTURAL BACKGROUND

The United States is unique in having the world's largest variety of ethnic and religious groups, most of them strangers to each other. This has often led to discrimination, harrassment, riots, lynchings, and even murder. However, in the 1990s the public accent has been on the positive side of multiculturalism. As a result, through education, children of varied backgrounds are coming together each day in nurturing classroom environments. In addition, textbooks are being rewritten to include the contributions of people other than white males. By means of equal opportunity programs, civil rights legislation, and public consciousness-raising, people of varied backgrounds are learning to work together in factories, corporations, government, and in the marketplace.

One need only look at popular culture and the arts to see hard-fought proof of population diversity: the presence of ethnic hosts and news anchors (Connie Chung, Bryant Gumbel, Bernard Shaw, Oprah Winfrey); African American situation comedies ("The Cosby Show," "In Living Color"); ethnic actors and actresses (Andy Garcia, Raul Julia, Eddie

Murphy, Edward James Olmos); recognition and widespread success of writers from other than white European backgrounds (Maya Angelou, Ana Castillo, Sandra Cisneros, Michael Dorris, Gish Jen, Charles Johnson, Maxine Hong Kingston, Spike Lee, Scott Momaday, Toni Morrison, John Okado, Ishmael Reed, Richard Rodriguez, Leslie Marmon Silko, Gary Soto, Amy Tan, Alice Walker); big audiences for musical groups such as Hiroshima and Los Lobos. Whereas once rap music was confined to African American audiences, it now claims listening enthusiasts from every segment of society. Other ethnic musicians as well have crossed racial boundaries to gather fans from everywhere, including Ruben Blades, Gloria Estefan, Julio Iglesias, and Carlos Santana. This listing of minority leaders represents only a few of those visible in the arts and media. Their success reveals the appreciation by the general public that all these voices are vital parts of the American chorus.

Perhaps the biggest breakthrough for multiculturalism has been the 103rd United States Congress. The candidates elected in 1992 represent the slow absorption of the multiethnic and female population into the power structure. The Senate totaled six women, one Native American, one African American, and two Asian American/Pacific Islanders out of its 100 members. The House of Representatives tallied 48 women, 19 Latinos, 39 African Americans, and seven Asian American/Pacific Islanders out of 435.

While many lament that these numbers do not accurately reflect the size of these lawmakers' constituencies, nonetheless they do represent a breakthrough in the formerly all-white male governmental leadership of this society. Add to this the rapidly growing numbers of female and ethnic judges, governors, mayors, and city councilpersons, and it is impossible to deny that change is taking place. Although this process has taken a painfully long time, it is still the most clearcut evidence that the acceptance of diversity is becoming a reality in this country.

CULTURAL RELATIVITY QUESTIONS

1. Have you ever had a disabled friend? Are you still friends with that person? Why or why not? What did you learn from that person?

2. Have you ever had a friend who was from a different religious group? Are you still friends? Why or why not? What did you learn from that person?

3. Have you ever had a friend who was born in a different country or who was from a different ethnic group? Are you still friends with that person? Why or why not? What did you learn from that person?

4. Have you ever had a friend who was much older or younger than you? Are you still friends? Why or why not? What did you learn from that person?

5. Have you ever had a friend who was smarter than you? Are you still friends with that person? Why or why not? What did you learn from that person?

LEARNING MORE

The following related topics may be explored: AIDS; cerebral palsy; epilepsy; blindness; deafness; African American heroes and contributions; Asian American heroes and contributions; Native American heroes and contributions; Latino heroes and contributions. Discrimination and racism examples: The Ryan White case (AIDS); KKK; Los Angeles Riots of 1992; internment of Japanese Americans during World War II; anti-Semitism; anti-Vietnamese fishermen activities in the Texas gulf; the Vincent Chen incident; the Zoot Suit riots.

TELLING YOUR STORY

Choose one.
  ▲ Tell about a time when you were the victim of prejudice because of your age, sex, physical appearance, religion, or ethnic background.

  ▲ Tell about a time when you discriminated against or made fun of someone because of their age, sex, physical appearance, religion, or ethnic background.

  ▲ Tell about a time when you met a person who was different than you are and you expected her or him to behave in a certain way, but the person surprised you (persons who are blind, homeless, old, young, handicapped, fat, ugly, beautiful, have a disease, or are from a different ethnic or religious group).

TELLING YOUR STORY VARIATIONS

Choose one.
  ▲ Create a poster that contradicts a stereotype. For example, show a person in a wheelchair playing basketball, or a blind person taking orders at a fast-food

restaurant. You can create a poster about the elderly, the handicapped, or a particular ethnic group.

▲ Pick a partner to role play a job interview. One person is the boss and one the applicant. The applicant tries to convince the boss that he or she can do the job. The boss should ask questions such as, "Tell me, why you think you can do this job well?" The boss should also challenge the qualifications presented by the job applicant.

The applicants should role play those who are commonly discriminated against—members of particular ethnic groups or the disabled in terms of physical, emotional, and mental handicaps. Applicants need to come up with some strong reasons why they would be successful at their jobs. Have the different pairs perform their interviews for the rest of the class.

TEACHING TIPS

"The neighborhood is changing" is a euphemism used when residents are alarmed about newcomers of a different racial or religious group moving onto their block. The euphemism expresses xenophobia, fear of strangers. Xenophobia is a universal phenomenon sometimes based on physical differences, as in the story about Michelle. Other times it is grounded in religious differences—for example, Hindus against Moslems in India; it can also be caused by language differences—French-speaking versus English-speaking Canadians.

Xenophobia can have dramatic and devastating consequences: hostility, terror, persecution, murder, war. However, people can overcome fear of strangers by turning those strangers into friends, which is exactly what Monsy did by sitting next to Michelle. Of course, it is unrealistic to expect to become friends with every stranger, yet at the very least, one can learn more about that stranger and reduce the foreignness factor. This is the first step; this is the challenge and opportunity presented in most American classrooms today. Remember that the classroom provides the environment in which students from diverse backgrounds learn to respect one another and live harmoniously, working toward the building of a common culture.

Remind students that many of their own ancestors came to this country because of persecution due to religious or racial differences. The treatment of Michelle is nothing more than reinstigating discrimination. That is why it should be unacceptable classroom behavior.

It is also shameful that through her silence, the teacher participated in the child's mistreatment by doing nothing about it. Fortunately there was a Monsy in that classroom.

Pay tribute to Monsy's courage to stand up against the crowd and protect her classmate. Talk about stereotypes (that Monsy and Michelle's skins were dark because they weren't clean) or the breaking of a stereotype (the students' surprise that Michelle was the smartest girl in the class).

If possible, you might bring up the delicate issue of parents who practice more stereotyping and discrimination than their children. Parents' multicultural exposure may be more limited, so for parents it might be more threatening to interact with strangers. Many students may be at odds with their parents on this issue. You can suggest that this is a common and very difficult problem. It is often impossible to change parents' opinions.

The point of the first Follow-Up Activity is that all things in nature are unique; even identical twins have differences. Do we focus on physical differences or human similarities? One has to look hard and see new characteristics, but the more one looks, the more nuances one can note.

The second Follow-Up Activity is a good way to examine if and how television promotes prejudice against certain groups. The questions asking how children would feel if they were a member of a group that was negatively portrayed allows students to hypothesize and empathize.

The purpose of the Cultural Relativity Questions is to demonstrate the risks and rewards of reaching out to those who are different. Through answering these questions students who have attempted to know others can be recognized for taking some risks and perhaps gaining some benefits while doing so. This may encourage others who have never done this. It is important to show how much we can learn from others who are different from ourselves.

By having students who have stepped out to embrace others share their experiences, they become models for their peers. If no student is willing to share an experience, then it might be appropriate to share some of your own experiences in this area.

In the follow-up to the second variation of Telling Your Story, those who play the role of job applicants will be encouraged to think of strong reasons why they can do the job.

Assuming the role of the stereotyped person should be of value in the future when students encounter real people who fall into these categories. Theoretically, it should help students gain respect for these persons' strengths instead of reacting with fear, disgust, or just sympathy for their problems. The person who plays the boss will be enforcing stereotypes. Afterward you might want to point out how easy and harmful it is to fall into stereotypical or xenophobic thinking and behavior. (Videotaping this activity could be valuable.)

SOURCES:

Kent, Corita, and Jan Steward. *Learning by Heart.* New York: Bantam Books, 1992.

Martinez, Jimmie, and Arlene Watters, eds. *US: A Cultural Mosaic: A Multicultural Program for Primary Grades.* 823 United Nations Plaza, New York, NY 10017: ADL of B'nai B'rith, n.d.